Queen of the Great Below

An Anthology in Honor of Ereshkigal

Compiled by Janet Munin

Dedication

H. Jeremiah Lewis

Hail to you Ereshkigal,
Great Queen of those below,
Mistress of the shadows, lady of bones and dust,
Frightening one of the far places where men fear to go,
Strong one who builds the boundaries and knows how to tear
 them down.
Ereshkigal, your magic is powerful,
and all the demons tremble in your presence,
doing all that you command.
Ereshkigal, you know the broken heart,
and the painful way to mend it.
Ereshkigal, you tear the layers from us,
hateful but necessary work,
as your whip brings purification through our tears.
Hail to you, terrible and revered goddess,
known from Sousa to Alexandria.

Acknowledgements

Janet Munin

I owe more than I can say the following blessed individuals:

Sara, my dear friend and teacher on the underworld path, without whom I might never have come to know Ereshkigal or embraced my vocation as a priestess.

H. Jeremiah Lewis, my first editor on this project, whose enthusiastic encouragement got it off the ground.

All the contributors who so generously shared their talents and their personal experiences, and who were patient during the years it took to bring this book together.

Rebecca Buchanan, the last of my three editors, whose encouragement and fine eye helped me reach the finish line.

LM, my partner, my lover, my husband, my king. . . Always and always.

And most of all: my daughter, the amazing person known as Wolfling, who has been loving and patient and courageous through my three years of grieving, and whose creativity is an inspiration to me.

Thank you all.

Table of Contents

Guide to Names

All names are Sumerian, unless otherwise specified.

Annunaki: The judges of the Sumerian underworld.

Dionysus: Greek god of wine, the theater, and ecstasy.

Dumuzi: A mortal shepherd, loved by Inanna. She married him and made him a king.

Ea: A later name for Enki.

Enki: God of crafts, mischief, and fresh water.

Enlil: Lord of the Wind. The chief deity of the Sumerian pantheon.

Ereshkigal: Ruler of the Sumerian underworld.

Erra: *See Nergal.*

Gugalanna: "The Great Bull of Heaven." Ereshkigal's first husband. He was killed by Gilgamesh's companion Enkidu while trying to defend the honor of Inanna/Ishtar.

Hecate: Greek goddess of magic and the crossroads, associated with the dark moon.

Inanna: "Queen of Heaven and Earth." Goddess of sex and war in the Sumerian pantheon, represented by the Evening Star. She was later called Ishtar.

Irkalla: A name for both the Sumerian underworld and its queen.

Kur: Literally "mountain." It came to mean both the underworld and a primordial monster that lived there who may have abducted Ereshkigal.

Namtar: An underworld messenger.

Nergal: God of pestilence. After first insulting Ereshkigal by refusing to honor her messenger, he was forced to descend to the underworld. Eventually he became Ereshkigal's husband and co-ruler.

Neti: Ereshkigal's steward, chief gatekeeper in the underworld.

Ninlil: "Lady of the Open Field." Consort of Enlil.

Persephone: Greek goddess of the spring who was abducted by Hades, king of the Underworld. Although her mother Demeter demanded that she be returned, Persephone had consumed six pomegranate seeds, and so had to remain six months of the year in the underworld and six on the surface.

Introduction

Janet Munin

Ereshkigal fixed Inanna with the eye of death
She pronounced the word of wrath against her
Inanna fell down dead
Ereshkigal had her corpse hung on a hook

For a great many people, this passage from "The Descent of Inanna" sums up everything there is to know about Ereshkigal, goddess of the Sumerian underworld: she is angry, jealous of her beautiful younger sister, vindictive, and vengeful. In literary terms, she exists primarily as the antagonist in the story of Inanna's Descent. In psycho-spiritual terms, she embodies the Shadow Self: all that is marginalized, hidden, and devalued within us. Do an internet search on her name and what comes up are primarily references to her as the villain of "The Descent" or lists of underworld demons. Academic research doesn't turn up much more. Ereshkigal is considered scary, mean, and dangerous – but ultimately a minor figure in myth and spirituality.

This devotional is a corrective to that perspective. Ereshkigal is not simply a bit player in someone else's story, and while "nice" isn't one of her attributes, there is far more to her character than rage and jealousy. She is a Goddess of Boundaries, refusing to be taken advantage of. She is a Companion in Grief, sharing the agony of losing a loved one. She is Goddess of Dealing With Your Shit, of facing all the things you would rather not admit about yourself, doing something about it, and becoming more than what you were. And yes, she is Mistress of the Descent: sometimes putting us through ordeals, sometimes simply there to help us through the inevitable dark places in life. She is one of the deities who operate the spiritual forges, those who help us be strengthened by hardship rather than destroyed by it.

In my experience of her, Ereshkigal is a tough but supportive boss who doesn't accept excuses or quibbling, but who is willing to answer questions and respond to arguments – and she is quick to give praise when it's been earned. She's not cuddly, but she is compassionate, in a tough love kind of way. She won't blink or flinch as she hangs you up on a hook, but she doesn't do it just for fun.

The Ancient Texts

Ereshkigal's Arrival in the Underworld

Ereshkigal appears in three different myths from the Ancient Near East, where she was worshipped from approximately 3000 BCE into the Common Era. The texts which have survived into the present are fragmentary, and there are different versions from different eras, but what we have is sufficient to paint a complex portrait.

The "story" of how Ereshkigal entered the underworld is briefly mentioned in "Gilgamesh, Enkidu, and the Netherworld." In the very first days of the world, the god An took the heavens for his domain, Enlil took the seas, and Ereshkigal ended up in Kur.

Samuel Noah Kramer, "the father of Sumerian studies," originally translated the phrase that described Ereshkigal's fate as "being carried off violently into the netherworld,"[1] and this continues to be the most familiar interpretation of the story. Kramer explicitly equated Ereshkigal with the Greek Persephone, a perspective shared by some of the authors of the Greco-Egyptian magical papyri who invoked the two goddesses together. More than one modern worshipper has also invoked them together, or as a conflated deity.

However Thorkild Jacobsen, an equally respected authority on Sumerian language and culture, asserts that Kramer's translation was incorrect. "The verb-phrase *sag-rig-ga-se. . . rig* does not mean, as Dr. Kramer translates it, 'to carry off as a

---

[1] Samuel Noah Kramer. *The Sumerians*. p. 114. First published 1944. Reprinted by Forgotten Books. 2007.

prize,' but literally 'to present as a presented present. . . . [a phrase used typically] of (1) votive offerings, including votaries presented to a deity, and (2) the dowry given to a woman at her marriage."[2]

Which interpretation is closest to the original may never be known. What we can say is that Ereshkigal did not begin as an underworld goddess, but once she entered that realm – called Irkalla or Kur – she never emerged again.

The Descent of Inanna

In this famous story, Ereshkigal's younger sister Inanna, goddess of sex and war, called The Queen of Heaven and Earth, decides to pay a visit to Ereshkigal. Her stated reason is to share the funeral rites for Ereshkigal's husband Gugalanna, The Great Bull of Heaven, but she is not welcome. Ereshkigal allows Inanna to enter, but as Inanna descends through each of the seven gates of the underworld she is forced to surrender a piece of her regalia. At the bottom, "naked and bowed low," she enters Ereshkigal's presence. Ereshkigal "utters the word of wrath against her" and "fixes her with the eye of death" and Inanna dies. Ereshkigal hangs her corpse on a peg, where it turns into rotting green meat. Inanna is saved through the intercession of her faithful servant and the god Enki, who creates two sexless creatures, the *kurgarra* and the *galatur*, and sends them down to the underworld. They find Ereshkigal on her throne, moaning in pain, and moan with her. Surprised and moved by their empathy, she asks them what gift they would like. They ask for Inanna's corpse. Ereshkigal gives it to them, and they revive Inanna with the food and water of life. Inanna ascends to the upper world, but must send someone down to take her place in the Great Below.

Ereshkigal's modern image and reputation are based almost entirely on this myth. She is portrayed as being jealous of her beautiful younger sister, and thus murderously bitter and vengeful. At worst, as indicated at the beginning of this essay, she is seen as little more than the villain of the piece, a foil to

---

[2] Thorkild Jacobsen in "The Sumerians: A Review," in *Philosophy, Religious Studies and Myth*. Robert Alan Segal, ed. Routledge, 1995.

Inanna's beauty, daring, and triumph. Those who look deeper characterize her as a symbolic representation of the Shadow, those parts of our psyches which we deny, bury, and try to hide, but which can burst out and cause terrible damage. Some interpret Ereshkigal as Inanna's shadow self, to whom she must surrender in order to be born again out of Ereshkigal's birth pangs.

Many Neo-Pagans use "The Descent" as the basis for rituals. In "Ereshkigal's Visit," "The Dark Mother's Mysteries and Lessons," and "Ereshkigal Speaks," Priestesses Inara de Luna and Belladonna Laveau have contributed powerful accounts of what they learned taking turns embodying Ereshkigal and Inanna in a series of large group rituals.

The Marriage of Ereshkigal and Nergal

The least well-known of the ancient texts are two versions of how Ereshkigal came to marry Nergal, a god of pestilence. In this story, the gods are feasting in heaven and Namtar, Ereshkigal's messenger, goes to heaven to bring back her portion, for she is unable to ascend herself. While he is there all but one of the gods rise to do him honor for his mistress's sake, but Nergal does not. When Ereshkigal hears about this, she flies into a rage and demands that Nergal be sent to her to be punished. The gods comply, but Ea cautions Nergal about how to behave in order to survive the experience. He must not sit in the chair that is provided, not eat or drink anything given to him, and not give in to the temptation of Ereshkigal's body. The young god follows the first advice, but sees Ereshkigal preparing to bathe and is overcome by her beauty. He spends six days and nights with her, then sneaks out before dawn and returns to heaven.

Once again Ereshkigal rages against the injury done to her and demands justice. She threatens to raise the dead to devour the living unless she is given her due. Nergal descends again, but this time as an aggressor. He muscles his way through the gates, barges into the throne room, and seizes Ereshkigal by her hair. In the earlier version, the two go straight to bed. In the later version, Nergal prepares to cut off Ereshkigal's head. She weeps, offering him a share of her sovereignty. Nergal, surprised, instantly relents, kissing her.[3]

Lee Harrington gives voice to Nergal's love for Ereshkigal in his poem "To Stay a Seventh Day."

The Perspective of a Modern Priestess

For many years, I knew Ereshkigal only from "The Descent of Inanna," and had absolutely no interest in her. That changed radically in November of 2007 when a ritual I was participating in took an unexpected turn and I ended up lying in the dust at the foot of her throne (see "Claimed by Ereshkigal"). Since then, Ereshkigal has been my patron, my teacher, and my mistress, and I've gained a far deeper understanding of her and her divine roles.

Goddess of Boundaries and Holy No

As I read and re-read the texts outlined above, I came to realize that Ereshkigal's frequent anger was always the result of someone else violating her boundaries or transgressing against her person. Whether it is Inanna insisting on entering a realm where she has no business going or Nergal refusing the gestures of respect which every other deity offer, Ereshkigal refuses to let others take advantage of her or insult her. When she seeks justice, as in her cry to the gods to return Nergal to her, even her threats are phrased in terms of proper boundaries. Unless they return to her the one who is rightfully hers, she will allow the dead to re-enter the upper world and kill the living.

Ereshkigal herself remains within her boundaries. As the ruler of the dead she is ritually unclean and cannot approach heaven, nor can she walk the earth. Despite the loneliness and burden of her position (which she also describes in her cry for justice) she remains where she is.

When I was in my early twenties, I wrote an essay describing Inanna as the Goddess of Holy Yes. She is always acting according

---

[3] It is not uncommon for later versions of myths to portray goddesses in more subservient roles to gods.

to her own will, always getting her way, always winning, always enjoying her sexuality. I have come to see Ereshkigal as the Goddess of Holy No. She is the one who helps us hold the line when others would take advantage of us. She is the one who encourages our righteous anger when our rights are violated, and who helps us say "I'm sorry, but no" when others ask for more than we can – or wish – to give.

The Goddess of Boundaries can also help us when we need to protect ourselves on the spiritual or psychic level, as Grace Barker describes in "Holding the Line."

Mistress of the Descent

There are two kinds of descent: the voluntary and the involuntary. Ereshkigal can be a companion and guide to both.

The involuntary descent occurs when we are rocked by the worst of what life can bring, when we feel overwhelmed and helpless in the face of problems that can't be fixed by a positive attitude or money or intelligence or friends. The descent can be due to the death or other loss of a loved one, injury or disease, employment problems, a dark night of the soul, or any of the countless other pains and sorrows of life. Ereshkigal can help us not just survive and endure these difficult passages, but find our way through to healing and transformation.

This was how I got to know her, as I struggled through three years of bitter grief over the death of my beloved partner. However warm the support of family and friends, nothing that anyone could say or do could bring him back from the dead or make it okay that he was gone. I raged and cried and screamed – and Ereshkigal was there with me, never denying my pain but always helping me to accept the initiation of his death and begin to build something new out of it.

The voluntary descent is undertaken when we realize that we need a radical change, and that nothing less will do than to strip away those things which bind us to the past, to the people we've been, so something new can emerge. This can be done ritually, as MasterAmazon describes in "Stripped to the Core," or in a systematic or radical lifestyle change. Ereshkigal is always ready to help us release or cut away that which no longer serves.

What is released goes itself into the underworld to be composted, consumed, and transformed.

Queen of Swords / Merciful Blade

In the language of tarot, the sword signifies the intellect, discernment, and decision. Ereshkigal's cool, penetrating gaze acts as a psychic sword, cutting through illusion and denial and laying open the truth to our unwilling eyes. She has no tolerance for self-deceit or clinging to outmoded beliefs, as Grace Barker writes about in "The Seven Gates," a vivid portrayal of Ereshkigal as the Goddess of Dealing with Your Shit.

In "She Comes to Me Masked," Clare Vaughn describes her as having "a surgeon's compassion and precision, cutting away that which must be removed, shedding blood of necessity and not flinching from her difficult, painful task. She has the compassion of the knife, her edge honed to cut cleanly when she strikes. Hers is the bitter healing, not the sweet."

In the tarot, the Queen of Swords is identified with the widow, the divorcee, and the spinster: women embittered by experience and grief. Ereshkigal has become associated with the negative stereotypes of such women: the bitch, the harridan, the harpy - but for those who are willing to listen with compassion and courage, she illustrates the power and dignity of truth-telling rather than pleasing.

Ordeal Mistress

Combining the roles of Mistress of the Descent and Merciful Blade, Ereshkigal as Ordeal Mistress is the patron of those who offer themselves up to extreme physical rituals in order to achieve healing, transformation, transcendence, and ecstasy, and those who preside over such rituals. Here she is most obviously a Bitch Goddess, using steel and rope, the whip, hooks, knives, and fire as sacred tools. She is a sadist who takes pleasure in inflicting pain on willing subjects, a priestess who makes a sacrament of the worshipper.

The Invitation

You now stand at the brink of the underworld, on the shadowed path that few walk willingly. Those who have contributed to this book have walked this road and returned again, bearing the blessings of the Queen.

I invite you to dare the path as well.

Ereshkigal awaits you. . . .

Are You Lost?

Janet Munin

Look around you.

Is this where you want to be?

This dark passage with roots and crawling things weaving in and out of thick, black soil?

Are you lost, little girl?

No way to go but forward.

Push on through the rotting leaves, the odds and ends of garbage, the things you'd rather not name.

Step over the stones and the beetles and the bones.

Has your hair ribbon caught on some sticks?

Leave it behind you.

Have your shoes become heavy with mud?

Go forward barefoot.

Don't think about what's in the muck that squishes up between your toes.

Time has no meaning here.

Throw your watch away.

Your dress is grimy and torn.

Abandon it.

Leave your pretty underwear too.

Make it a shroud for some small animal's carcass.

The ring on your finger does not shine in the darkness.

Cast it back into the earth from which it was made.

There is no room here for excess.

You cannot pass save in your own purest form.

Ahead, the passage widens.

Light flickers across earthen walls.

You hurry forward, into the light, into the open.

Into Her presence.

Here are all your nightmares made flesh.

Here is your only hope of salvation.

Fall on your knees.

Offer praise to the Lady of the Great Below.

Your descent has only begun.

Darkness Rising

Sophie Reicher

I praise the darkness,
in which the Great Queen awaits.
I praise the devastation,
and Her precious gift of tears.

I praise the moments
in which She takes me up:

each lash, each hook, each rending talon.
I am laid waste: a feast for Her children.

Perhaps Neti will record my passing.

I praise the magnificence of Her kindness.
I honor the gift of Her love;

for it is only by the lash that my ego may be tamed.
It is only by hook and flensing knife that the poison of my own bitterness
may be cleansed from my heart.

It is only through the harshness of Her compassion
that I may be raised up out of soul-ruin and barrenness.

So ever shall I praise this Goddess of the Great Below.
Her blessings are endless, Her mercy vast,
the gift of Her grace mighty.

Irkalla

Melitta Benu

I was swallowed by the gaping maw,

The dragon's mouth.

I came and conquered.

Rape could not break me,

Darkness could not silence me,

Here in endless eternity

I have set the stones

Of the kingdoms of the dead.

I created a throne from his bones,

And covered my nakedness with his carcass.

Though I thirst for clean water

And mourn the childhood play that was never mine,

I am the Mistress of the House of Dust.

To me all things must return

And from me will never be parted.

I am the Final Justice.

I am the one who ensnared the heart of Nergal,

She who is warmed by the heat of war.

I am the one for whom

Erra shattered through the seven gates

Seeking the softness of my ebon mouth,

His heart's dearest desire.

I slew Inanna, and hung her corpse as a trophy on my wall,

And I alone held the power to return her,

to release the radiant one from darkness,

to free love from death,

to allow the shaman's return from the Great Below.

To me, the dead come

With empty eyes and hollow hearts,

Eating the primordial mud,

Returning to it,

To the place where all things began;

To the place that I have become,

the dust my breath, the earth my body,

the darkness my spirit, my name

whispered through lips pallid with dread:

Irkalla.

To Stay a Seventh Day: Nergal Sings to Ereshkigal

Lee Harrington

Touch me my love and lie with me
Touch me my love and be my mate
Six days shall we lay, my love
And on the Seventh I shall not flee[1]

Long ago my love my father came here
Long ago my father and mother came here
My father your father's first born
And the man that made your father shed tears

*

You could not come to the feast, my love
You could not be there in the flesh
So I knew not the shame I did, my love
And I would not bow before your minister

*

Namtar whose name is Fate saw me
Namtar whose name is Fate told you, my love
He took this shame back to your ears
And I knew I would have to make amends

*

I went to your brother Ea to ask
I went to your twin of Magic born in tears
His laughter erupted as I told him my folly
And he shook his head at my pride

---

[1] Each time the * appears, return to the first stanza for a repeating chorus.

*

He had me make a throne of sacred woods
He had me heed how not to stay seven days
To eat nothing, take nothing, leave nothing
And warned me never to lie with you

*

So with his blessing I made a throne
So with his blessing I descended the stairs
I asked Namtar to admit me at the gate
And he shook his head at my pride

*

I brought you gifts to make amends
I brought you gifts to show you my power
For I am the god of War and Pestilence
And I thought to stand sovereign before you

*

For I am a Prince born of Enlil and Ninlil
For I am the Justice of the Gods on Earth
So I stood before your sovereign throne
And turned away your hospitality, my love

*

You took from me the throne, my love
You took from me my loneliness
As I sat with you and talked, my love
And found in your skin my equal and more

*

I gave into my heart's desire, my love
I gave in to you and did what men and women do
We embraced each other, my love
And went passionately to bed

*

We lay there, you my Queen and I
We lay there for a first and second day
Together our flesh and sweat mingling
And our moans and laughter echoed loud

*

Queen of the Underworld you took me in
Queen of my heart you conquered me
We lay there for a third day
And our hearts sung out to every shadow

*

My love, you opened up to my lust
My love, you opened up to my joy
In the land of the Dead, Justice and Memory
And we lay there for a fourth day

*

We found in each other a mirror
We found a way to abandon loneliness
We lay there for a fifth day
And acknowledged each other's strength and love

*

Together we lay for a sixth day
Together we whispered and smiled
Finding strength in each other's skin
And fell asleep spent in each other's arms

*

Waking before you, my love
Waking before you in the dark I sat
Remembering what Ea had told me
And became afraid of staying forever at your side

*

I crept out on swift and silent feet
I crept out like the lurking death I spread
Fleeing into the night I snuck from your bed
And ascended the stairway back to heaven

*

Namtar came to you, my love
Namtar came and told you of my folly
Your faithful vizier came to you as you woke
And your rage shook the earth above and below

*

They say you cried out aloud grievously
They say you fell from your throne
Straightened up from the ground and wept
And tears flowed down both your cheeks

*

But I could hear nothing of it
But I could think of nothing but my fear
I was afraid of giving in to love and life
And could not believe I had found both below

*

In short time Namtar came to the heavens
In short time he brought your words to us
That you were a woman of complexities and power
And I came to the hall to hear what he had to say

*

I heard him speak of your childhood, my love
I heard him speak of your loneliness below
Of your power as Queen of the Underworld
And your rage in my behavior for how I left

*

The Gods all then looked to me
The Gods all shook their head at my folly
Oh Nergal, they sighed and pitied me
And each pressed the case for and against you

*

Finally I sat alone with my thoughts
Finally I sat and thought of you, my love
Six days and nights I conjured in my mind
And remembered just what it was that I had left

*

I remembered your smile and moans
I remembered the way I felt at your side
Then sat and tore my hair knowing I needed you
And cried at my pride and arrogance

*

Twice now I had insulted you
Twice now I had shamed myself
I did not know that you had sent Namtar
And did not know he took those tears back to you

*

I caught myself in a mirror, my love
I caught myself and saw my soul for a moment
In that moment I saw what you had seen in me
And I knew I could be all you saw and loved

*

Descending the stairs I let go of my folly
Descending the stairs I let go of my pride
Namtar stepped almost smiled as I passed
And allowed me into your chamber unannounced

*

For by Dakuni what is above is below
For by Dakuni our love will echo on every plane
Oh my love, forgive me and love me again
And together we will soar

*

Let me be your king at your side
Let me support you in your greatness
For you have shown me the worst I could be
And you will always show me the best I am

Touch me, my love, and lie with me
Touch me, my love, and be my mate
Six days shall we lay my love
And on the Seventh I shall not flee

Touch me, my love, and lie with me
Touch me, my love, for a first and second day
As our flesh and sweat mingle together
And our moans and laughter echo out loud

Touch me, my love, and lie with me
Touch me as you conquer my heart
We will lay here for a third day
And our hearts will sing to every shadow

Touch me, my love, and lie with me
Touch me and open my lust and my joy
In the land of the Dead, Justice and Memory
And we will lay here for a fourth day

Touch me, my love, and lie with me
Touch me as we both abandon loneliness
We will lie here for a fifth day
And acknowledge each other's strength and love

Touch me, my love, and lie with me
Touch me and whisper and smile
Find strength in my skin as I find it in yours
And we sleep spent in each other's arms

Touch me, my love, and lie with me
Touch me, my love, and be my mate
Six days have passed as we lay, my love
And on the Seventh I did not flee

Stripped to the Core: Ereshkigal Frees Inanna from Religious Bondage

MasterAmazon

For me personally, the Dungeon has always represented the Underworld, actually and metaphorically. Some interpret it in the 'evil' or negative sense; thus energetically I cannot be in the midst of those kinds of scenes. It is a matter of intention. Partly why I enact these scenarios is about both the pain and pleasure which conventional society hides and denies, and 'cutting through': getting down to our true erotic, physical, emotional, spiritual, naked Selves, both our Dark sides and our Light sides . . . .and the magical ability to transmute pain to pleasure, or release shame. That is what this whole ritual was about: purging, releasing and letting go of religious indoctrination, control, and sexual shaming; then embracing sexual and spiritual empowerment and freedom.

I met her in the mid 1990's. She was emerging from six years of celibacy within her Church and coming out again as a Lesbian. More than a decade beforehand she had gone back into the closet, and she had been completely celibate during the last six years after she converted to Mormonism. I don't usually date those just coming out as Lesbian, only those who are rock solid in their Dyke identity. So I interrogated her about her decision to reemerge after many years of denial. She stated she was *very clear* she was Lesbian and wanted to *fully express her lesbianism*, and wanted *nothing* to do with her religion any longer.

She had grown very disillusioned with the religion, especially once she realized how patriarchal it was. When she took her one year Mission she realized it was one big salesmanship game to recruit souls and money for an already rich Church. She found there is no room for overt homosexuality within the Mormon

Church, as its support of California's Proposition 8 (outlawing same sex marriage) has made quite clear.

She wrote the Church and asked them to take her "off the rolls," which meant voluntary excommunication. She wanted to plan some kind of ritual to celebrate her excommunication and her freedom from that Church. I began to study their theology, doctrine and even rudimentary magic. The more I read, the more experiences she shared with me about their rites, the more heavy handed and absolutely patriarchal the system seemed to be, snuffing out any creativity or power of women especially.

I picked up a slim book on the Inanna myth and read it. I also reread Lesbian author Judy Grahn's work *Queen of Swords*, which is a Lesbian reenactment of the Inanna myth. In Grahn's version, Helen, presented as a modern housewife, slums one day and enters a Lesbian bar and meets "the Butch of the Realm," Ereshkigal. Helen endures the same events that Inanna does, but with a modern day Butch/Femme twist to it. Since my partner and I were in a Butch/Femme relationship, this worked out for us. I really could relate to being the "Butch of the Realm," hanging up Helen/Inanna on her peg and putting her through three days of trials before she could emerge. . . much like the Dark of the Moon.

The energy of my Top space, especially in connection with ritual, is somewhat akin to the severity of the Crone/Dark Goddess. There is a simplicity in my dress, all in black and black leather generally, representing knowledge, as in the Black Belt I possess, and the Zen-like simplicity and 'cutting through' nature of the martial artist. I use Sadomasochism/Sex Magic as a technique to shed layers of being cloaked from one's naked Self, to cut through, both physically as in rending garments, and metaphorically. I *feel* Her severity -- the TaskMaster, the Zen Master, the Master Instructor, the plain spoken, direct gazed, non-codependent, non-people-pleasing Dark Goddess/Crone -- She is part of me as I Top. It may not always be Ereshkigal; it could be Hecate, Medusa, or the severe part of Artemis as well. In the ritual to come, I as Ereshkigal would lead my partner through a Rite of Passage to let go of the shame and all else that oppressive religion had burdened her with. Through physical, emotional, and psychic means she could release that burden as she was stripped and passed through the Gates to meet Ereshkigal.

My partner finally received her notice that she had been dropped from the rolls. We burned the notice ritually. We prepared for several months through study and ritual to re-create the Inanna/Ereshkigal rite at a local women's play party near the Spring Equinox, which I felt was the most appropriate holiday. Spring Equinox is a very powerful holiday energetically for me, since it is easiest then to shed the Darkness of Winter and emerge into Spring, as Persephone does to then be joined with her Mother Demeter, the myth I usually reenact on this holiday. This would be a different focus, a different myth, though similar in certain ways. In this case, my partner was emerging from the dark winter of six years under intense patriarchal religious authority where she sacrificed her Sexual being, and she would be coming into Spring, reclaiming that part of herself, and Ereshkigal would be her guide to shed that control over her, through the passage into Spring.

I wanted my partner, who was new to Goddess worship, to understand the awesome act we would be undertaking, to read the myth of Inanna and Ereshkigal herself, to be fully ready, and to know that this was *real*. I wanted her to be very clear that once we did this ritual any vestiges of Mormonism would indeed be swept away.

The night finally came. I wore my usual black leather and black garments. I had my knife at my side. My partner dressed in her white Mormon Temple garments: a white dress with many layers beneath it. The outfit included a green apron, representing the fig leaf that Eve wore, the last layer, but she would not put that on until we were ready to begin the Rite itself.

We had not told anyone at the play party what we were going to do; it was a secret between us, and as we interacted with the other women, nobody suspected a thing.

Finally, it was time. She put on the green apron. I hung her upon the St. Andrew's Cross, then began to strip her, cutting off part of the garments to reveal her back. I began to flog her slowly, then built up the intensity. This was a Rite of Passage; as each garment was stripped off her, she passed through another Gate, shedding that which she no longer needed, until finally taking her over the threshold through the pain and intensity of the flogging, the naked rawness, to meet the Goddess Ereshkigal, Goddess of the Underworld. Using my knife I slowly stripped off the rest of her garments till she lay naked upon the cross. The last item to go was the green apron, the fig leaf, and along with it, her innocence.

It came to me during the Rite that the role Mormons and other Christians would see me as would be the Christian Devil....that part scared me. But as I've been into Goddess Worship for many years, I *refused* to take that role, and their judgments, on...I could feel those judgments as a very real force. Instead, I affirmed strongly the matriarchal role and Power of the Goddess I was embodying...the Dark Goddess Ereshkigal. I would much rather be judged by Her, a female entity, who I personally believe because she is Female, ultimately has compassion underneath all Her sternness, not the destructive and deliberately cruel patriarchal other. Realizing this in these moments that the Goddess has compassion, especially towards other women, I held and nurtured my partner after working her over. This flash of insight came to me in those sacred moments and I truly realized that what we had done was immensely powerful.

Now she was rid of the physical vestiges of Mormonism through the rending of her sacred Mormon garments, and hopefully she was freed of the psychological and spiritual controls as well. Little did we know just how well this ritual worked.

What the months and years of our relationship later revealed was that she did not replace the Void left in her life where her Mormon spirituality had been. We had a women's circle that met every other month at our house, and she could create beautiful altars and art reflecting female and Goddess images, but it seemed she could not take the Goddess on...or allow anything else inside her. At first I thought these were my biases, that she wasn't moving along the Path quickly enough, or that it was her stubborn personality, but there were others in our Goddess circle who saw the same things. All the forms were there, but not the substance. She had experienced a real break with *any* connection to a Higher Power . . . and does to this day.

This is my one regret. Ereshkigal really *did* help her let go of Mormonism, but there was a Void that was left in that space, a Void she never replaced with Goddess or with another benevolent Higher Power or system, even though she participated in all our rituals. Instead there was a glass wall and an attitude of "nobody is going to tell me what to do or how to believe". Our relationship ended in 2001 with an ugly breakup. A mutual Pagan friend told me recently that my former partner has gone towards atheism, which saddens me. The ritual indeed worked, but neither of us knew the full outcome. There was a part of me that felt guilty and filled with regret...and yet....we both had agreed and consented and did all the work to prepare together.

Perhaps Ereshkigal's gift to me was the ability to take on the role of Funerary Priestess several years later when those close to me passed, and also the ability to continue to communicate with them on the Other Side through my dreams.

I still have great respect for Ereshkigal and Inanna, but if you work with Them be prepared for the outcome. It may not be what you expect. It is a Myth that is true in its essence that taps into very powerful and *real* forces.

The Space Before Her Throne is Strewn with Broken Eggshells

Janet Munin

we come before You
clutching our
precious fragile brittle lives

bodies minds and spirits
drawn tight
curled up
desperate to protect
what we know we are

in Your holy presence
we crack
we shatter
we are torn open

screaming
bleeding
weeping
the broken fragments
of our illusions
drop unheeded to the ground

and we discover
in our raw newness
the beauty and power
we had kept hidden
in our own shadows

Stonebreaker: A Call to Gugalanna, Bull of Heaven

Lee Harrington

Monster in my bones
Beloved of my first tears
I hear you breaking stones
I hear you breaking stones
In my heart

Gugalanna in my bones
Bull of Heaven in Kur
I claim the fear and woes
I claim the fear and woes
In my heart

I battle monsters
Each day
I battle you my sweet
Each day
I battle my reflection
Each day
In the shadowed lands of Kur

Monster in my bones
Beloved of my first tears
I hear you breaking stones
I hear you breaking stones
In my heart

We each need a first to open us up to our potential, to pave the way for future tales, to shake us from our comfort zones. In Gugalanna, Ereshkigal found that first husband, the Bull of Heaven, who came to Kur and paved the way for her own future, the Mistress of the shadowed lands of the dead and more, she who was strong enough to take those lands when no others would and yet not strong enough to love or cry fully. This call to Gugalanna is a call to find a breaker of stones in your own life. Not to be taken lightly, this call asks for someone to shake us from our comfort zones, slay our dragons, show us a mirror to our potential and find us a pathway to our own road through life. Be mindful that this may take many forms, and can manifest in astral aide, internal dialogue, or an actual individual who will come temporarily into our lives and shake our world or manifest into this role then leave, not always in the easiest way. For strongest calling force, consider doing this in a dark mirror, in a mirror in a darkened room, or under the auspices of the new moon.

Claimed by Ereshkigal

Janet Munin

Even now, three years later, I vividly remember what it was like to be sacrificed: naked, blindfolded, chained by my neck and wrists to the sacrificial rock and abandoned for the gods to do with as they pleased. My heart still beat, my lungs continued to draw breath, but for all intents and purposes I was no longer a part of mortal human life. Eventually my body would give out, succumb to dehydration or exposure or even the cruelly merciful touch of a divine hand, but that would be a formality. My existence as a living woman was over.

This was not the experience I had sought or expected when my lover[1] and I planned the ritual of binding and sacrifice. Although we had always used the term "sacrifice" in our discussions, what we had in mind was more a temporary consecration of me as his priestess-agent, one who would offer up prayers on his behalf, represent him before the gods and perhaps serve as their oracle to him, and then be returned to my normal life. And yet, despite the explicitness of that intention, our actions and invocations had turned me into something else entirely.

At the time of the ritual I had been on the path of the underworld priestess for perhaps four months. The death of my lover had devastated me, but it had also been the gateway to a powerful initiation. A relatively new friend had reached out to me in her own role as an underworld priestess and offered her service and support in my grief. The more I learned about her

---

[1] The lover I refer to throughout this piece is LM, whose death triggered my underworld initiation. His participation in this ritual was entirely in spirit. Trying to fully describe the experience of working with a disincarnate partner would draw the focus from my encounter with Ereshkigal, so I have glossed over those details.

path, the more I began to feel as if I had finally found my own calling. Not only did the symbols and ways of working resonate with me at a deep level, it held out a possibility that nothing else did: that of continuing to have a relationship with the man I loved.

The ritual we designed together was, at the most fundamental level, one of binding. It was a way of practicing the magical skills I was learning, practicing working with him in his spirit form, and a way to spend focused, dedicated time with him. The stated goal of me acting as a priestess on his behalf was less important to us than the steps leading up to what we continued to call the sacrifice.

Those preliminary steps of binding, marking, and offering up were extremely powerful, extremely intimate, and the details are not something it would be appropriate to share in this context. Suffice to say that by the time I was naked, on my knees, blindfolded, and chained by neck and outstretched wrists to the headboard of my bed, I no longer felt like my own person. I had voluntarily surrendered all that I was to my partner, who had in turn fully rendered me up to the gods.

There is a dual consciousness that takes over in such situations. My rational mind was fully aware that I was alone, on my bed, restrained by bindings that I had placed on myself and could easily undo. My magical awareness was of something entirely different. I was not in my bedroom. I was half-hanging from a large rock that stood out beyond human habitation. I could not get up and leave at any time. I had been given up to the gods, and there was nothing I or any other mortal could do about it

My mouth was dry. In my pre-ritual fantasies, this had been the point where I started to pray -- first for my lover, and then as the spirit moved me. In my fantasy I was eloquent, filled with the power of prophecy. Now that I was actually stretched out in my bonds, words failed me. I whispered a prayer for my beloved, and then tried to pray for peace. But my words, though sincere, fell like pebbles onto dry earth. I finally realized that prayer was not to be part of my purpose – and I certainly was not going to play the romantic, powerful role of bound oracle.

I was simply a sacrifice: a naked woman, sundered from all her former connections, bound to a rock and waiting to die.

Not what you expected, eh? came a crackling, edged, amused voice -- and I knew Hecate was with me.

No, I confessed silently. *It's not.*

Can't be a death priestess if you haven't died, she told me briskly. *Of course, you've already died, many times – but you don't remember.*

This is what being a priestess is, she told me: *a sacrifice to the gods, dead to all but the will of the gods. "Hierodule" you've called yourself, "sacred slave" – this is the truth of it: naked, with a chain around your neck, the gods' slave. You do their work, not your own. You don't worry about what anyone else thinks or wants. You mind your masters.*

Yes, I thought.

Hollow bone, she reminded me – invoking a concept from my shamanic training: being the hollow bone of the flute through which the wind/will/music of the gods pass.

Grail Chalice, empty, a conduit. . . No place for all that other stuff to get in the way, muck up the Waters.

You just hang here a while. There's no place for you to go.

I had the sense that this would be longer than I wanted, but not nearly long enough to rate as a true ordeal. We were not set up for that. But this was a descent – not what I had planned, but voluntary. The voluntary descent was something I hadn't done in a very long time, was something that needed to happen as part of my underworld training.

I needed to remember that as a mortal I am already dead – but that the gods have brought me back again and again to serve their purposes.

I was to feel myself dead, know myself dead, find that place of after-death where all the memories and identity and connections are gone, and hang there for a while.

I won't pretend that I fully achieved that place of non-being, but I brushed up against it, passed into and out of it, more than a few times. Time stretched out. I did my best to keep my consciousness focused on the inner world, to forget the objective truth of my safe and comfortable bedroom and the realization that my bent and bound legs were becoming numb. I was dead.

Eventually Hecate drew me back from the abyss and took me down a long, dark, bare path into the underworld. Fully committed to the process, I was allowed to release my wrists and unwrap the end of the chain from the head of the bed – but only if I collapsed and lay as one dead on the bed/altar. I obeyed, and felt my right leg start to tingle as circulation was restored. Hecate mocked my bound-shut legs. My sex magic, life-magic, could not function in my dead body.

We reached the bottom of the path, passed through a large, featureless gate, and I was tossed -- bound and on my belly – into the dirt at the foot of Ereshkigal's throne.

How to describe that moment of looking up and first beholding Her?

I have been blessed with a mystical aptitude that has allowed me to enjoy deep communion with the divine in various manifestations. In virtually every encounter, I have experienced the gods as warm, supportive, welcoming. Ereshkigal was none of those things. She loomed above me on Her throne, huge and beautiful and terrible and stern. She was dressed in elegant robes of midnight blue and deepest black. Her hair was black and Her skin was starkly white. There was no welcome in Her gaze, no warmth in Her expression. I felt like a dead mouse dropped by a cat: something to be coldly amused by and then kicked into a trash bin. I was ashamed of my smallness, of my naked helplessness. Then She smiled down on me, and I became truly frightened. Her smile had a knife's edge and no reassurance at all.

She reached down and pulled me up by the chain necklace-collar, so my face was directly in front of Hers, her fingers curled around the chain. "You wanted more depth in your spiritual practice," She said, smiling her terrifying smile. "This is where you go deep."

Most of what She said after that was and remains private. The most important thing was that She was aware of my desire to be an underworld priestess, and She was willing to take me as Her own so I could learn from Her. The price was my death, and lying naked and prostrate in the dirt while she conducted business. I was to be dead and accept it, understand it. The world was lost to me. (And in quiet counterpoint to her cruel voice I heard whispered reminders of all that was dear to me, all that I should cherish and embrace when I was returned to life – although so deep was my sense of being at Ereshkigal's mercy I wasn't entirely convinced She would ever fully let me leave her throne room again, never truly embrace life as a living being again.)

She affirmed my sense that I was to become a teacher. I was to teach the truth as I understood it, and not to worry about what other people thought, since I would be teaching for the sake of the gods. The chain around my neck was no longer an accessory for my lover and me to enjoy in our play, it was Her mark on me, Her reminder to me of my status as Hers, and I was to wear it when I taught as a priestess. *Your cunt belongs to LM*, she acknowledged, *but your ass is mine. You're my bitch. You wear my collar.*

Dead, naked, bound at the foot of her throne, hearing Her offer me what I've wanted, but in terrible form, all I could do was agree.

And you'll wear this chain for the rest of the day, to remind you. Wrap it twice around your throat, and feel my presence.

Yes, I said. *I will.*

Satisfied, She told me I was free to go for now, and left the throne room.

I continued to lay helpless on the floor, aware that I did not have the power to rise from where I was and that my lover was barred from entering the underworld to come after me.

Then Dionysus was at my side, offering me wine to start reviving me. Persephone was there a few moments later, beautiful and serene, offering me a pomegranate. *You can eat it,* she assured me. *You already have the power to go in and out of the underworld.* Their sustenance brought life back into my body.

At some point during this transition, I heard Ereshkigal's voice and saw something like a smile – an expression with which I would become very familiar in the months ahead. *You have to be a bitch first, before you can become a Bitch Goddess.* It was a reassuring promise of blessings and growth to come. She seemed amused, a bit pleased. Almost not scary.

When I was alive enough to re-enter this world, my lover was at my side. Working as quickly as possible without being chaotic,

I removed bindings. I tried to undo the chain to re-wrap it according to Ereshkigal's demand, but couldn't work the toggle clasp. Finally I gave up. I left the blindfold on, since I wasn't yet ready to be confronted with the living/waking/material world.

I am going to fuck you back to life, LM told me with his fierce-tender tone. I was very cold, so I cuddled down under my blankets. He began to touch me, giving me his fire. I warmed up quickly, and my desire for him also came back from the dead. We came together as husband and wife – loving partners, no ritual left but the chain collar around my neck to remind us both that I was fresh from the underworld and still bound to its mistress.

* * * * * * * *

In the three years since that day, I have come to know Ereshkigal well. The chain collar has been replaced by a beaded necklace which I made on the day of my initiation as a priestess. I no longer kneel in the dirt, but stand before Her as her cherished servant. I still see Her knife-edged smile, but I have also known her tenderness. As I finish my work on this devotional, I am looking forward to a new ritual with Her, one of rededication that will reflect my growth as a priestess in Her service and the changes in my life that have come with the healing of my grief. I remain rooted in the underworld, but as a living being it is important that I balance those energies with those of the upper world.

I was afraid at first of moving away from Her, but She has let me go with grace. Our bond is still there, but I spend less time in Her presence.

"You have to release even Me," She told me quietly. "I am your patron, and I will still be with you, but you must continue to move forward."

The ways of the underworld are perfect. I do question them sometimes, but I never doubt the love and faithfulness of my Queen.

Hymn to Ereshkigal II

Rebecca Buchanan

Great Lady Under the Earth
Mistress of Irkalla
When Nergal stormed your realm
     daring to claim it for his own
You lay with him
In your palace of lapis and bone
     and so won his heart:

Queen of Kur
     soon
     you will own my heart
     too

The Bones of the Earth

Older than time, I Am.

Older than the animals,

Older than the plants, I Am.

When the Earth was still aflame with star-fire, I Was

When the first vapor rose, as the sludge sank, I Was

When the Bones of the Earth were forged, I Was.

I am not the river, I am the bed that cradles her in her courses.

I am not the ocean, but she rose from my womb

I am not the fruitful Earth, I am the dark matter from which it

propels itself into light.

I am the plates of stone sliding across each other

I am the Memory of the Earth

I am Older than My Name.

Samhain, 2004. A coven-sister created a Sabbat ritual focusing on the Descent of Inanna. The rites included poetic "sermonettes" by Inanna, Dumuzi and Ereshkigal. Our lead priest and priestess were to officiate, calling in Inanna and Dumuzi, and I was asked to evoke Ereshkigal.

I had lots of experience working with Inanna. During the early 90's I was inspired by the Qadesha work of Tara Webster, and spent years engaged in a monthly and seasonal practice of devotion, chanting, and libation to her and Ishtar. This was synchronous with many of my magickal colleagues who began playing in Inanna's current around the same time. However, the connection for me eventually faded once I had integrated what she wanted me to learn. I continue to be intrigued with the mythology, and have created and attended several rituals based on the myth of the Seven Gates. It's a powerful and resonant story. But when I was asked to evoke Ereshkigal, I realized that I had never really acquainted myself with her. The speed with which I got to know her shook me.

Within hours of receiving the first draft of the ritual, Ereshkigal was Present. Her energy was palpable, and distinctly foreign to me. I'm no stranger to chthonian Goddesses, but Ereshkigal was unlike anything I had ever encountered. The feelings and images were immediate, but words to name them came slowly, and with effort. The first word was "depth". Caverns and caves and rock strata descending ever further into the alien world beneath our reality. Spans of time so vast my mind could not conceive of them. Through it all I felt she was holding back, knowing I couldn't take the full weight of what she was. She kept saying, *I am not the river, I lay down the bones of the river's bed.* My dreams became very vivid but I remembered nothing the next morning. And I had a mad craving for potatoes, lentils, and beans: hearty Earthy fare.

My coven mates and I emailed revisions and changes back and forth; we would not have time to meet until ritual night itself. The ritual became more elaborate, more formal. There were to be spoken word pieces by the three deities, then a walking meditation through seven "gates" where we had to give up a token of what we'd leave behind on the descent. Each of the four ritualists – three deities and one psychopomp – were working on our parts at home, informed by the collective working but individually following the current where it took us. Ereshkigal wanted altar space. She chose bones, wood and shells for her space. I felt moved to fill an antique silver bowl with dirt from my yard. She wanted soil and dirt, with chunks of coral below the topsoil. On this I laid out my seven tokens to charge up prior to the ritual.

The night of the ritual, just as I was driving into the driveway, my Priestess called. She was sick, too sick to come, and would I mind presiding over the ritual? I was happy to do it, and did the honors perfectly, except for one thing: I was supposed to call in

Inanna at the beginning of the ritual. Although I cleansed, cast circle and called the quarters just as we had scripted, when it came time for me to call in Inanna, it slipped my mind completely. I called in Ereshkigal instead. The ritual went on fine – no one noticing the change except for my coven-sister who wrote the ritual. At dinner afterward she whispered "You called the wrong Goddess, silly!" But I hadn't. After the work I'd been doing for the past many weeks, Ereshkigal was my only thought, and to have called in another Goddess, even her own sister, would have felt wrong, would have been wrong.

After Samhain, Ereshkigal faded away. She had nothing more to say, and once I dismantled her shrine and returned the rocks and coral to the garden, she was gone. I have not heard from her since then, but now, when I drop my energy into the Earth to ground, I feel like I go deeper, into places I could never reach before. In times of stress and worry, my core is strong and unshaken. I surprise myself at times with how much stronger I am since Ereshkigal's brief visit. I feel this is her gift, and I honor it.

Naked and Bowed Low

Janet Munin

I entered the throne room naked and bowed low

Understand, you who listen

I did not say *broken*

I did not say *tortured* or *beaten* or *shamed*

I entered unencumbered

I entered in humility and gratitude

I entered in awe and adoration

I laid my head in the lap of the Goddess

I bared my throat to the Bitch of the Great Below

I surrendered myself to the Queen of Irkalla

For the knife edge of Her mercy is my salvation

And in Her fierce love I embrace eternity

Drawing the Line

Grace Barker

Ereshkigal. Queen of the Great Beneath. Goddess of Boundaries. Her hair is a darkness that hasn't seen light in longer than we mortals could comprehend. Her skin is alabaster stalagmite that spears air holding the metallic taste of ore and the tickle of damp moss. Her eyes gleam like a pool of water that glows from within, an echo of a sun-kissed day miles out of reach. This is the goddess I see when I speak to her: stillness and shadow that is always there, ever-watching, ever-lasting.

I do not work with the goddess often, or at all, if truth be told. My Master is of a different pantheon entirely, although they both share the bailiwick of Death in different manifestations. As such, there is a certain acceptance, a knowledge that, should I need help, I will not immediately be turned away. The goddess will at least listen to my words. Whether she helps. . . well, that is a different matter entirely.

One day I did end up needing her help. I had set the circle, but the work had drawn the attention of ones who were not welcome. I drew the power of the Grey Lands between life and death about the circle as a deterrent, but the darkness was not afraid. I drew the fire of life, hid it in that deep shadow, and that seemed to confuse them for a while, but eventually the darkness I defended from did manage to pass.

If death could not turn away the darkness, and life did not deter it, what did I have left? I didn't know, but then I remembered the goddess of boundaries, the Queen, and I reached for her. I asked for her help to hold the line. In the broad light of day, I saw the entrance to her kingdom: a small arch into a stone mountain that led to a winding path. From experience, having walked that path, I knew it spiraled and turned deep into the earth and ended in a cavern so grand that it seemed to have no ends or limits. I knew the gates that stood between the shadowy palace in that awesome space. But standing just out of the touch of daylight, far above at the entrance of this path, was the goddess, Ereshkigal. I had asked for help, and she had honored my plea.

I told her of the obstacles I had placed, and I asked her to help me hold the boundaries, to stop the darkness from passing through. She smiled at me, her beautiful mouth turning in a grim amusement sharp as a dagger's edge. "You don't need me to hold the line," she said. "Forbid them entry and it shall be so."

I was sure I had not heard correctly. Who was I to stand before the darkness and refuse them passage? I hadn't the power to do that.

"Draw the line in the sand," she said. "Will that they shall not pass that line, and no force at their disposal can slide by even a touch."

I didn't understand how I could hold against the darkness without her help, but I did as she had told me, and was surprised when the line held and my grim determination kept the darkness at bay. I won't say it was easy, but it wasn't the effort I had thought it would be.

The duty passed, the mission ended, and the circle was removed. All seemed to go smoothly. In my confusion, I sat down and spoke to my Master, not understanding the greater lesson in Ereshkigal's instructions. How could I hold them back? I really didn't believe I had it in me to do that.

"Belief" was the answer I received. The line was mine to draw, and my will was inviolate. There was no way the darkness could pass if I went beyond belief to *knowing* that it could not, simply because I said so. Fear made me balk at the idea that my word could have such power. What if I was wrong? What if I made a mistake? What if the thing I fought was powerful enough that my will didn't matter? Obviously if I stood before Ereshkigal (or any other god) and forbade her entry, she would be more than capable of swatting me like a fly, so how could my will hold other beings out?

Knowledge is a powerful and frightening thing. When one *knows* something, then there is no possible way for that to be wrong. If you know that the sun will rise in the East, then obviously where the sun rises is East because there can be no other way. This is beyond faith, beyond belief, to a place where there is no room for doubt. The power that was explained to me was a frightening thing, because it so carefully walked that thin, shining line between truth and self-delusion. That way lays madness.

Yet. . . I believe it. I have not worked myself up to knowing, because I am not ashamed to admit I have doubts, and I'm afraid of the implications of what I've been shown, but I believe it. This was the word of Ereshkigal, the Shadow Queen of the Dead, and this was the kind of deadly gift that one would find in Darkness.

Let Me Be Burned in Thy Sight

Callista Evenstar

Ereshkigal
Mistress of the Underworld
I am Thy Handmaid.
Open Thy ear.

Ereshkigal
Who casts aside the veil
Who strips away the veils
Who destroys the veil of illusion
Thy Handmaid would approach Thee.

Let me be burned in Thy sight.
Let me be consumed in Thy sight.
Let the scales fall from my eyes.
Let me be transformed in Thy Holy Fire.

Take from me the seals of temporal power.
Take from me my material things.
Take from me my concern with material things.
Strip from me the veils of illusion,
that I may see clearly and be renewed.

Ereshkigal,
Mistress, Destroyer
Strip me
Change me
Cleanse me
that I may be reborn.

She Comes to Me Masked

She comes to me masked. Always, the background color of the mask is a stark matte white. Patterns of red, or red and black, overlay the white. The shape and style of the mask and its patterns change: most often oval; sometimes a truncated oval, like the masks used in Greek tragedies; at other times large and in the likeness of a shield. In addition to the paint it may carry decorations of fur, feathers, pieces of tanned leather. The facial expression of the mask ranges from flat and lifeless to enigmatic to exaggerated and distorted. But always, the background of the mask is white, the patterns red or red and black.

She takes the mask images from my mind, from memories of museum visits and art history studies, as a way to communicate to me both her nature and the limits of our relationship. I am not one of hers, nor is she one of mine; she comes to me to help me teach one of her priestesses, to seek my help in passing on what cannot be spoken directly. We have an uneasy truce, she and I, not suited to one another nor bonded in any direct fashion yet working together for the good of one close to us both.

She carries the whiff of the underworld, this goddess of the realms of the dead. She carries also a fierce wildness and a sense of distance, distance with an edge in it: the edge of a razor. This goddess carries scars and knows how to inflict them, not through viciousness but through need. She is an ordeal mistress who works with a surgeon's compassion and precision, cutting away that which must be removed, shedding blood of necessity and not flinching from her difficult, painful task. She has the compassion of the knife, her edge honed to cut cleanly when she strikes. Hers is the bitter healing, not the sweet. Hers is the bed of pain from which one rises shriven. Hers is the sharp cleanliness of carbolic acid and poke root, remedies which burn as they cure. Hers is the harshness of a desert hermitage, the austerity of locusts and wild honey and no water left for tears. Hers is the alchemical fire which transmutes suffering into gold, whence falls away the ashes of all that she would have you shed. The healing she gives is the healing of loss and release.

She is not a goddess of mercy. Hers are not the soft pillows, the silken robes, the easy tasks, the motherly indulgences. Hers is the strength born of trial. Do not call her lightly, for she will change you and the cost will not be small. Her gold comes at a high price. But if you are hers, the price is worth the purchase, for your soul needs her touch. If you are hers, seek her fearlessly. She will answer you with truth as her blade amputates what you must surrender.

As I edit this for final draft form, she stands behind me. She knows what I have written, and the mask she wears today – a curved heraldic shield – shows a fierce smile. I have the sense that she is pleased with my words. I offer them to her, for it is on her behalf that I have written them.

Ereshkigal as The Queen of Swords

Shirl Sazynski

The Oracle of Ereshkigal

Galina Krasskova

My voice is heard in the howling of the damned. Those who suffer invoke Me. Bitterness is My throne, loneliness My salvation. Bring Me these gifts and I will teach you survival. I am the Black-faced Queen of the Kurgarra. I have been forgotten in your dark places, the secret surfaces of your hearts that gleam like obsidian mirrors. But I am there. My jewels, My treasure-box are those things others discard. I get the last, the least, so I learn to draw blood from shadow and I claim the bones.

Cry with Me. Touch that darkest, barest place within your hearts. I am loss that scalds the flesh. I am envy and jealousy and hate, and I am all that lies beyond. Madness is sometimes My gift: they are like Me, the ones who have often seen too much. I mend again the shattered heart. I turn it to a field of glass. My breath is the darkness that brings the cold chill of fear. I have known love but it has not known Me. I teach patient endurance.

I am the Opener. I take your pain, misery, barrenness and loss and with it weave My cloak. I am the Barren One and I collect what others do not want, all the things that make you see beyond the prisms of day's illusion. I hallow the heart.

I am the One Who does not touch. Seek Me where your loss is greatest. I am beauty that scorns the light, lonely beauty and bitter rage. I collect the fears you release. You mistake Me and My place—darkness is not barren. I am Mother to monsters, all your hidden fears, and I teach you to master yourselves. I lead you to light.

I am beyond death. Pain is pleasure too for what it teaches. Light without darkness is nothing at all. I am the Goddess no one wants but all must seek. I am the Mother of all loss. I make sacred the spirit. Fear is My greatest gift to you for courage is a dark blade whose honing must be earned. Bring Me offerings of wormwood for it is bitter like My heart. I am the Eater of Corpses, flesh is My feast. I am the ash that remains from the offering. My gifts and My treasures are many to teach but I must be invited in.

At the Gates

Erynn Rowan Laurie

The Gatekeeper poems were written as an expression of a mysteries ritual where the initiate passes, living, through the gates of the Underworld to meet its unnamed ruler. The names and characteristics of the gatekeepers are derived from syncretized Egyptian and Sumerian models.

1. NEDU

i watch as you approach

you
      in your arrogance
living

my skin shifts
bones and muscles twisting
      what face shall i wear to bring you fear?

you who live
      this is not your place

i scratch your name in the wall
lost among billions of names
who have passed this way before

your name is the first thing you lose

2. ENKISHAR

even gods have felt my sharp fingers
between their ribs
tearing

what need have you for heart or lungs
        here?
no breath escapes your lips
        even now
no name
        binds you to the world

spill your blood here
among the echoing caverns
their walls have seen rising floods
        oceans
now dried brown

you must be hollow to enter

3. ENDASHURIMMA

life is shit

you think you'll walk away but
if you pass my watch you'll be
        gutless
        twitching
intestines glistening
strung from stinking walls
strewn as offal on the path

you've had your last meal
i know what you ate
the smell of your fear
the dark earth of your shit
my food

you have no lungs to scream

4. ENURALLA

                    who
who are you child
            child

who are
                child
                        ild

                                ild

hollow
        like bones sucked of marrow
                        marrow
                echoing

without name
        you come
without heart
        you come
without bowels or lungs
        you come

and i will tear away
        your voice
        your tales
        your songs
i will take them for my own
        to join my choir
                                choir
                choir
        yes
when you are silent
        then only
you may pass
        may pass
                pass

5. NERUBANDA

your flesh decays
        food for worms
your very shape is lost
consumed

57

and i consume what eats you
wiggling
wriggling
falling away
fat with your flesh
      it is the perfect circle

what muscle is left stands here
      trembling
before my polished gate
thin, bloody shreds on bone

my gate is black obsidian
finer than Ishtar's blue enamels
      what you see reflected
is body-truth
writhing

worm-food
i will swallow you

6. ENDUSHUBA

none who pass this way return

empty within
empty without
i take what sustains you

no breath
no pulse
no voice

no food

you starve for light and bread
      and music
you starve for warmth and beer
      and incense

i take the grain of your soul
    you cannot sprout
    you will not rise
    the yeast of your hope
            dies
    in my hands

your drying bones rustle
desolate
as you pass

7. ENNUGIGI

your dry bones click
and rustle
on the path

you may go no further
    nameless
    breathless
    bodiless
    lifeless

i will carve your bones
hollow your thighs to flutes
sever your joints with my blade

sharp obsidian
        marks
what's left
whittles bones to lace

flecks of bone dust fall
like snow at my feet
drift in the slow dark air

only your dust may pass

The Seven Gates

Grace Barker

It was through a shamanic journey that I first decided to meet with the Queen of the Great Beneath. I had long considered Her, having heard things of Her that intrigued me, especially "Mistress of Thankless Tasks." It had not occurred to me that a goddess could be perceived with such a title, and let's face it, which of us at some time or another have not felt the need to pray at the altar of One who would understand the never-ending drudgery of menial labor, customer service, and the care of hearth and home?

But it was not as such that She presented herself to me. This title had been suggested by a person I did not know on a website that I couldn't find again. Though it intrigued me, I didn't want any man-made epithets to stand in the way of my understanding of what She had to say to me. So, with my guardians and allies by my side, I found the tunnel into the Great Beneath and started to make my way down.

The tunnel was dark, though I could still see my way clearly. There were no torches or glowing lichen or anything else along the way that would account for my ability to see, but of course such things are not always necessary. It felt cold, the chill in the air almost damp, though the walls and ground were perfectly dry. The tunnel was not smooth, but seemed like a large creature had burrowed the man-size hole as it made its way into the deep below. It wasn't long until I came across the first of the gates.

My original vision of the gates dates back to a mythology class in high school, where I first heard the tale of Inanna passing into Ereshkigal's domain. In my mind, Irkalla was a tremendous cavern deep within the earth, the back of which could not be seen, and the seven gates were crafted walls around the palace of Ereshkigal. Presumably these gates melded with the wall at some point so that the rest of Irkalla lay beyond the great palace. The gates were fairly close together, and the gatekeepers were figures in black robes, deeply cowled. This was the vision I was presented with upon entering the dark realm. When I reached the first gate, I was informed by the gatekeeper that I had to give up one article of clothing.

This was when my mind rebelled. I couldn't possibly be having this as an actual journey. I was merely mimicking what I knew of the story of Inanna's descent. It was so cliché I wanted to turn back or change the journey somehow. However, I was reminded that though it may feel contrived, it didn't make the journey any less real. So I gave the gatekeeper arm bangles I wore and moved on.

I experienced the same request at the second gate, then of course at the third – and here I was stalled for a long moment. I didn't wear an awful lot of clothing in my journeys and I didn't really think I had seven things to give. More than that, it felt wrong, like I was making this up. Doubts crept into my mind. Speaking to Ereshkigal was supposed to be an exploration of the self, or so my mind told me. How then could I find the answers I was seeking by going outside myself through journeying? Shouldn't I go within, through meditation? I spent a long time debating this, attempting to turn back, stepping again toward the third gate, and generally prancing in place like I was trying to talk myself into knocking on a cute guy's door for a date. Eventually I managed to calm my mind, telling myself it couldn't hurt to at least finish the journey and to see what the Goddess had to say. So I gave the gatekeeper the hair piece I wore.

The seventh gate ended up being tricky, as I tried to consider what I had left to give, but eventually I passed through, into the palace of the Queen, visions of hooks dancing in my head. I really did not want to hang by my heels, thank you. I hardly remember anything of the dark palace except that the walls were black as the moonless night – but then I was before the great goddess. To me She was vastly beautiful and wearing blue satin, probably from an image I had seen of her. Her skin shone and her hair was glossy and as black as her palace. She sat upon a great throne, looking down upon me, and demanded, "What took you so long?"

I blinked up at the queen. "I . . . well . . . I wanted to make sure the time was right, that I was ready."

"You were lazy," She said. "You should be more prompt. I've been waiting for you. What is it you want?"

I wasn't prepared for such a quick and blunt dressing down, and struggled to bring myself back to my purpose. "Your priestess is arranging an anthology of works for You, great Queen, and I wanted to honor You by participating. However, I didn't know what kind of work to do. What would you have me write in Your honor?"

"You will write of your descent," She said. "For seven days, you will explore the gates of the Great Beneath and learn what these gates are in your heart."

"You want me to write about myself?" That seemed highly unnatural and uncomfortable. I didn't want to talk about me.

"You asked, didn't you? That's what I want. Now, since you're here, you can work until the incense burns out. Go to the first gate."

Not entirely sure what else I should do, I turned around and left through the seven gates, reclaiming my clothing. I spent a long time trying to decide how to go about it. Did I disturb my neighbors with my continued drumming, or did I settle into a meditation? In the end, meditation won out. I returned to the entrance of the tunnel.

The First Gate

As I re-entered the tunnel, I found my guardians gone and Ereshkigal at my back. This did not concern me, as I knew they were watching, and though the Great Lady intimidated me, She did not frighten me. I never worried for my safety with Her.

I made my way down the tunnel to the first gate. Strangely, the schematic of Irkalla seemed to have changed. The gate was not part of a built wall, but a door closing off the tunnel. Fortunately, this time I did not have to disrobe, probably because the Queen was with me.

"This gate," Ereshkigal said, "represents your passions." Inside the gate there was very little to be seen.

"You have little passion," the Goddess said, and oh, how it hurt to hear this and know I had to write it down for others to read and bear witness to. My mind immediately began wandering to pen names I could use so that no one would know who had actually written this piece. A clear sense of impatience brought my mind back to where it was supposed to be.

"You have things that you believe in, but nothing you avidly support, nothing you wouldn't squeak by on with convenience."

My mind first went to my job. I didn't believe in cruelty to animals, but the medical research institute did animal experiments. Part of me truly believed that it was the only way to develop these cures, but another part of me worried over the quality of life of these poor animals. "But it's my job. I don't work directly with the animals, and it has taken me years to find a job that pays so well with such excellent benefits."

"Alright," She said. "What else?"

"I love wolves," I said, somewhat timid at this point.

"Have you done anything to support them? When they were removed from the endangered species list, did you protest?"

"No," I said softly. "I keep meaning to, but I haven't sent money yet."

"What of your writing? You love to write, but you spend your time not on your stories, but on pretending to be someone you are not with another person."

"That's social interaction," I protested.

"You need friends."

"I have friends. They live an hour away."

"You need closer friends," She said patiently.

"I hate parties and that's all friends ever want to do."

"Do you see my point? You make excuses as to why you cannot fight for what you believe in. You are lonely. Why do you not seek to end that?"

"I'm focusing my energy on my practice," I said, pitifully close to sulking.

To my surprise, the Goddess leaned in then and kissed me. "I know," She said. "You temper your passions so that others will not mock you for them. It is a shield. You only show your true heart in humorous ways so that no one will take you seriously. It is the only way you express what's in your heart."

She stopped our walk and pointed to the wall. There was a small trickle of liquid, a tiny waterfall in the otherwise featureless domain of the first gate. "One day, that waterfall will gush with all the passions in your breast, and it will become a great river, one to be reckoned with."

I must admit, I felt doubtful and silly. A strong part of me felt that I was making this up. Why would a goddess be calling me a passionate and lonely creature? Still, I could not ignore the 'feel' of the meeting. I knew in my heart that all I was being told was true, even if my head still occasionally felt the need to mock it.

"Now, turn around and grab your laptop," Ereshkigal told me.

"Grab my laptop?"

"You need to write this all down."

"Are you sure? Am I just trying to get myself out of an uncomfortable situation?" I asked.

"Grab the laptop."

"But—"

"Grab the laptop now."

The Second Gate

This time I met the Goddess just inside the tunnel and She walked down with me, easily moving past the first gate.

"So, I have a question for you," I said to Ereshkigal as we walked. "What exactly am I supposed to do with the knowledge you're giving me? I'm not sure how to implement it."

"What of the book you have been reading?" She asked. I had, for about a month, been working my way through *Urban Shaman* by Serge Kahili King. The chapter I just finished talked about taking on those traits that hinder one's shamanic practice.

"Adding more passion was not one of the listed topics."

"Ah, but procrastination was, and guess what we are reviewing today?"

By this time we had stopped before the second gate and I let out a long-suffering sigh. "The second gate is procrastination? Shouldn't that be one of the latter gates since it's such a huge problem?"

"The second gate covers a larger area."

"Good point."

The gatekeeper stepped aside and the Lady led me into the new area. It was cluttered with piles of just things littering the entire area. There was no rhyme or reason to anything and it made me feel quite a bit guilty.

"Recognize it, do you?" Ereshkigal asked, Her tone sly.

"I'm too tired to work on this," I said. I'd had a hard, tiring day at work and hadn't even wanted to do any meditation. I knew it would make me think and, quite frankly, once I get home I don't want to do that.

"That's my point," She said. "You don't spend enough time working on the things you should. You don't want to clean, or cook, or to do the practices assigned to you. These tasks are not such difficult things if taken a small bit at a time, but you ignore them and let them build up. You should not do this."

"So what's the moral of this?" I asked. "I mean, procrastination doesn't hurt anyone, so why make an issue of it?"

"It hurts you," She said firmly. "You do not care for yourself, and it makes you uncomfortable and builds the walls about you even higher and thicker. Do you see how easy it was to just push past your weariness and simply do what needs to be done? You did not want to meditate today, but you did, and now you have one less thing to worry about. If you can do this consistently, then your burdens, which weigh you down now, will ease."

Ereshkigal turned away and began to walk through the piles of things that littered the second circle of this Great Beneath. I hurried to follow Her, sensing that things were not yet finished. "So, what would you have me do?" I asked, unsure still how to implement what She was telling me. "I mean, this is a big problem for me. What do I *do* about it?"

"A little at a time," She said. "When you get home, don't put off the things that need to be done just because you're tired. Just do a little, and eventually it will add up. Clean a few dishes, put away some of your crafts, do a bit of exercise and, in time, you'll see results."

"But I don't have time," I said, tired. "I have to go to bed earlier now for that project at work, and I barely get home, then have to meditate, then make dinner, and spend at least some time unwinding, then suddenly it's bedtime."

"Well, first, you don't need to take so much time in the morning."

"I won't have time to eat breakfast any more, and speaking of exercise, I'm losing that time as well."

"Ah, but now you can throw together something simple. A fruit smoothie is healthy and nutritious and won't take you long to make, plus you can take it with you for travel," She said sweetly. "See how well that works out?"

I almost hated to admit it, but She did have a point.

The Third Gate

I walked down in to the tunnel with the Goddess, past the empty rooms of the first gate and the cluttered mess of the second. The air seemed warmer this time, more like a spring day. I smelled damp earth and wondered what I was getting myself into.

As we approached the third gate, Ereshkigal looked sideways at me, smiling in a way that was almost wry. "What do you think will be behind the third gate?"

"I didn't know before," I murmured, bemused. "As I settled myself down to do this meditation, I wondered what it would be, but now my intuition is telling me its logic."

"That's right," She said in approval. "Quite frankly, my dear, you think too much. Do you understand why this might be bad?" With a gesture, the gatekeeper opened the way, and we went inside.

The interior of the third gate appeared similar to the climax of the first Matrix film. I could see green lines of data running down the stone walls, casting everything in an almost sickly green glow.

"Too much thought hinders the intuition and makes it difficult to just be in the moment and feel," I replied. I felt rather quiet and distant as I looked around. This was a problem that I was aware of. Often in meditations, I cannot sit silently and just be. There must be some kind of visualization or action to accompany my mind. "Our society values intelligence and thought."

"And displays so little of it," She replied. "It's not that people are unintelligent. It's that you all become so hyper aware of everything and process all of your knowledge in everything that you do that the most simple ideas, like locking the door to your car or, simple details like the differences in regular blood and a sample that's been chemically treated, become lost in the mix. Yours is a society that spends too much of its time trying to survive in an overwhelming environment. You can't even enjoy the erotic facets of your nature without over thinking things."

I looked around sadly. This was certainly true. "How do you get around it? I mean, even now, I'm typing while meditating."

"It's important to remember that you're doing it to more accurately do what I commanded of you," She replied.

"Still, how do you get around this overabundance of information and still survive? Better yet, how do you just stop *thinking*? I don't know how to accomplish this, and I've tried."

"Another thing your society has implanted in the minds of its people is instant gratification. You think that because you cannot do it now, or even in a week, that you have failed. Think back to the spell work you were analyzing this morning. You performed a spell last year at your Yule holiday for more money. You saw no results and thought nothing of it but, six months later, you were promoted. Things take time. You cannot have everything you want right away."

"But what if it feels like it's too hard to handle without it? For example, I want to pay off my credit cards now."

She snorted rather inelegantly, or as close to it as such an awesome being could. "So does everyone. Do you think they all should? You had a bad habit, and now you are suffering for it. That difficulty does not just go away because you want it to. How would you learn?"

"But if everything is a lesson, how can we avoid overanalyzing?" I asked, rather shrewdly I felt.

"It's one thing to analyze the events once they have happened, quite another to do so while they are still happening. You must live for the moment. Reflection Analyzing should be done as a daily practice. Until then, enjoy each breath, for as you know, they are limited."

There was a truly sharp smile on Her face as She said this, Her white teeth shining in the blue aura of Her presence. It wasn't sinister or anticipatory, but certainly edged, and all the more chilling for it. Who would know better the precious frailty of life than the Queen of the Great Beneath?

The Fourth Gate

I started at the tunnel and made my way down. Almost immediately, Ereshkigal appeared behind me.

"You blogged about Me today," She said, amused.

"I think it was yesterday, but heck yeah. That comment of Yours was a bit chilling."

"My priestess' question to you of your acceptance of death was wise. You should consider this with your Master."

I nodded, the intention of having a discussion with my Lord already in my mind. "I will do so, but back to the topic at hand."

"Ah, yes," She said. We passed through the first three gates easily, the buzz in each becoming less noticeable to my mind. Less significant. I questioned Her about this.

"It's because you acknowledge each area as a problem. Though you are not yet active in finding solutions, your spirit and hindbrain are working on the problems."

It was then that we appeared before the fourth gate, the wraith-like gatekeeper and stone door no different than the previous three.

"Have you an idea what is behind this gate?" She asked me, looking sideways at me with Her dark, dark eyes.

I frowned. "I had an idea this afternoon, the random thought just coming to me. And now. . . are You telling me the answer, or am I intuitively getting it, because my thoughts are saying 'body image.'"

"It is your own thoughts, not I telling you. These are the gates of your soul. You know what your areas of improvement are," She said, giving me a sideways, almost disapproving look as I am reluctant to use the word 'problems'. Being told I have problems by a goddess seems far too negative to me, and She picked up on that.

"It is not like being told by a peer that you have a problem," She said. "It is more as if the alpha bitch has told you that there are areas you need to improve in. If they hamper your progress in your journey and spiritual path, they are problems. Now, stop thinking about Alcoholics Anonymous and enter the door."

With that lovely command, how could I now not think of standing before a crowd of amorphous beings and stating, "Hello, my name is Grace, and I have a problem"? I said nothing out loud, however, mostly because I knew that She knew what I was thinking – and we passed through the doorway opened by the fourth gatekeeper.

Inside this section of the gate were mirrors. They were all flat, but all seemed to emphasize various parts of my body, and not in particularly flattering ways. In this regard, it felt much like a fun house.

"Yesterday, you told your sister that there was nothing gross about self-love, and there was certainly nothing gross about her body, yet you have such a negative view of your own body. Why is it that you have such double standards?"

"Everyone does," I murmured, looking in the mirror that showed my physical body as it really was, and not the spirit body I have taken these journeys in. My shape made me uncomfortable.

"Why does it make you uncomfortable?" She asked softly from behind, Her eyes focused on my naked form in the mirror.

"Because. . . well. . . I don't think it's gross," I said quickly. "But sometimes it *feels* gross. Love handles where rolls of fat rub against each other. . . It's not a good feeling."

"Then work on it," She said. "It's as simple as that. If you are uncomfortable in your body, do something about it. If you must be someone's bitch and obey commands about what to eat and what not to eat, that's okay. Sure, it's better in a feel-good fuzzy way if you can acknowledge that you don't need to have external rules, but you admit to yourself that you can't, that you operate better under those rules. So do it. Imagine a master who would give you these orders. Ask your real Master to give them. Ask your spirit lover. Just don't ask me. I'm not your diet coach," She said, almost primly. I had to laugh.

The Fifth Gate

I made my way down the tunnel, leaving my guardian behind me at the entrance. The first stretch of the tunnel was empty and the gatekeepers silently opened the doors as I descended. I felt the great Queen's eyes on me, but She did not appear to me yet. I continued down until I arrived at the fifth gate. Strangely, the gatekeeper opened the door and he let me pass.

The area behind this gate was smaller than the last. Each progressive zone has become smaller and smaller. I didn't believe it was because the problems were becoming smaller and smaller, but that they were deeper and more intense, shadowing everything that came before. There was hardly any light in this room, just enough to barely see. There was no sound, no features. The room was barren and empty and almost oppressive, and I saw that the fifth gate represented loneliness.

I knew Ereshkigal was there, observing the lesson, so I started to wander around. There was, of course, nothing to see. I sort of found this an unfair problem to be presented with, honestly. I live alone. I am allergic to cats and most likely have become allergic to dogs. I have no mate, and when I ask about it, am told firmly that one would just distract from the lessons at hand. I am too tired to spend much time with my friends after work and have little time to do so besides, especially considering the practices I perform once I get home, so what is this about? How can I fix a problem like this?

I suppose there is a possibility of a companion/familiar, but I perform no magic, so maybe just a pet. Then again, a familiar could help me use magic to help the world and my community, to share loving and healthful energy with them all, but this is beside the point. A pet is not something I can afford right now, and I'll be moving in with my sister soon anyways, so what is the problem? Why is this being pointed out to me?

Is there a further need to spend time with my guides and guardians? Sure, that can be done, but it doesn't take away the desire for physical, real contact. What exactly is expected of me?

There is no answer.

The Sixth Gate

Once again I was left to make my way down the tunnel alone. Ereshkigal awaited me at the sixth gate, the gatekeeper a shadow compared to Her glorious presence. "I think you know what is inside this door," She said to me.

"Anxiety," I said. I wondered if it would be the sixth or the seventh gate.

"I think you already know what the seventh gate is, and it's the worst of them all, but let's not venture so far just yet." She nodded to the wraith of the gate, who opened it, allowing us to enter.

The area inside the sixth gate was painfully similar to Munch's *Scream*. Horror and an endless wail seemed to fill every corner as the walls ran in crazy, epileptic colors that made me cringe. My entire body tensed.

"Anxiety is a demon you have tried to battle before, and she bit back hard," the Goddess observed. "She will be a great adversary to you, but you have thought on this issue before."

"I'm aware that my anxiety is an issue for me," I said, looking around with a certain amount of trepidation and wariness. "Using the chuh, or feeding my demons, was not an easy practice to try. It nearly caused me a panic attack."

"But now you have the tools to try again. Easing your anxiety should be a meditation of calm and peace," She said. "You do not bottle up the anxiety and force it from your mind, as you so often attempt to do. Acknowledge it. Understand its control over you, then allow it to pass from your mind. Bottling it up inside just allows it to crawl from your gut and up your throat whenever it sees fit. You master nothing in this regard."

I nodded, looking around the place. "So that's it then? It seems like such a powerful demon."

"She is," the great Queen said. "But she will not defeat you if you have strength, and you must have strength. If you did not, I would not be wasting my time with you. Also bear in mind you should not create anxiety, either. Do not allow the idea of what others think about you to cause anxiety where none existed. If the person matters, they will accept, and if they do not accept, then they do not matter. It is a cold view, but that's what separates the queens from the peasant girls. You are a priestess. You are a goddess in your own power. You must know this, live this, and let no one tell you what to do with it. Besides, of course, those who have that right, and you know who they are.

"You stopped me from using the word 'understands' instead of 'accepts,'" I pointed out. "Why?"

She gave me Her chilling, edged smile. "Because you are woman, and are Mystery. No man, nor one who does not walk in Mystery, should ever understand you."

I found myself returning Her shining, white smile with a dark smirk of my own.

The Seventh Gate

I left my guardian again at the entrance of the tunnels and made my way down, this time with great trepidation. So far, I had journeyed through six of the gates of Irkalla and all six gates had led me somewhere painful and difficult for me to deal with. I had thought my anxiety was the root of the problem, but no, I still had one gate left. I didn't know what this gate led to or what would be behind it, and I was worried.

I passed down through the first six gates, ignoring the contents of the gates as they tugged at me, and approached the final gate. It looked no different from the rest, with the great Goddess standing next to it and the gatekeeper in silent attendance as usual.

"Are you ready for your final challenge?" Ereshkigal asked me.

I sighed, looking at the stone door, then nodded.

"Have you any idea what this is?" She asked me.

I considered the door for a moment, thinking. "I don't think it is a challenge, is it?"

She smiled then, graciously, as if I had pleased Her, and nodded to the gatekeeper. He opened the door and, beyond it I saw a large, dark palace or temple.

"Your palace?" I asked.

"Yours," She said. "This is your heart, the center of you."

"What?" I said, confused. I studied the temple, moving slowly closer. "I don't understand. I've been to the temple that is me. It didn't look like this."

"You've been to the temple that is your body. This is your power. And thus we come to the final challenge between you and the temple doors."

"Power?" I asked nervously. But it's so dark. . . "

"You are surrounded by beings who walk in death and shadow," She replied. "Did you think your power was air and light?"

"But I don't have real power," I said. "I just do what I'm told."

"And thus the final challenge is humility."

"How can humility be a challenge?" I asked, so confused.

"Because your humility borders on self-defeatism. You are never excellent, never the best, never wonderful or admirable in your own eyes."

"Because I'm not the greatest," I said. "There will always be someone better."

"And that's a fine thing to know. However, that doesn't make you any less excellent or awesome. You are not just a servant, you are a Priestess. You do not just listen, you are a Shaman. You walk between the worlds of dream and shadow and you have many powerful beings by your side who are fond of you. Humility is a great thing, but you have the power, and you must be unafraid to wield it. And on that day, when you can accept that you are beautiful, and awesome, and powerful, then you will complete the final challenge and step through the doors of your temple. That is when the real work will begin."

"How can I do that?" I said, tired. "It seems like there are too many things that get in my way."

"That is what life is about, little one. It is about challenge and obstacle. You cannot be complacent, or the tide will sweep you where you had no desire to go. You must be active in discerning your fate, or how can you be the guide of others? You are the torchbearer, the one who wanders the darkness with lantern held high to guide those who cannot see and are overcome. How can you do this if you fear the light going out?"

I swallowed, looking up at the beautiful temple. "How do I resolve these challenges?"

"They will take work. Some I will help you with, for others you will have other companions. You are never alone, but you must do the work. If you rely upon others then it is not your power you will find, and the seventh gate will always stand in your way."

I gave my thanks to the Queen of the Great Beneath, asking for any final instructions. Her words were brief, and I left Irkalla and headed back into the light of my sacred home. Once outside, I embraced my guardian and considered what I had been shown and how to begin the tasks that had been laid before me. It would be challenging, but I had no fear of failing. The tasks laid before me were challenges to reach the depths of my own being. How could I fail to be myself?

Smoke rises, weaves its dance
In the shadow of the greatest deep
Queen of all that hides Beneath
Command me through that endless sleep

Her Mirror

Sophie Reicher

He is Her mirror,
quiet to the maelstrom of Her power,
serenity and ice to the raging blackness of Her fire.
God of plagues, and war, and passing,
He knows the sweet gift of eternal release.
Only with Him might the tumultuous power
of Her heart be eased.
He is Her sanctuary,
this God of devastation,
this Warrior Who knows too well the weary price of peace.
Only He is brave enough to dare Her power.
Only with Him, might She find ease.

Welcome to Irkalla

BellaDonna Oya

Ereshkigal sits in her lapis hall, weeping and wailing...
My husband has died, my only love, and even I,
The Queen of the Dead, could not save him.
I am alone now... All is sorrow, all is death!

Inanna sits on the Throne of Heaven, wondering...
I, the Queen of Heaven, know life and love,
But I do not know death and what comes after.
I will visit my sister, she will teach me.

What? SHE is coming to Irkalla?? Why???
She who lives in the light and beauty of the stars,
Why does she intrude upon my sorrow
When she cares nothing for my pain??

I have come to visit you, my sister.
Your husband died to avenge my honor,
And now I wish you to teach me of death
So that I can mourn with you in your sorrow.

How dare you think you can mourn with me,
You who always think only of yourself?
My love is dead, and it was for YOU he died!
My heart is broken, but you hear only your own desires!

Why are you so cold and angry?
The Queen of Heaven must know all Her kingdoms,
And understand the cycle of life.
Teach me of death, my sister, so that I may understand.

Yes, I will teach you to understand death...
Are you happy now, my sister, now that you
Hang as dead meat from a hook on the wall?
Now do you understand MY kingdom??

Who is coming now to disturb me?
Why will no one leave me alone in my misery?
All I wish to do is mourn my love in peace,
But no one cares for my feelings, my sorrow.

Oh, my heart! Oh, my liver!
Oh, Her heart! Oh, Her liver!
My husband, why did you leave me!
We weep, we mourn for the Bull of Heaven!

Who are you, why do you mourn with me?
We heard your cries, alone here in Irkalla.
We are come from Heaven to comfort you.
Can this be? That others care for my pain?

I thank you for your kindness to one in need,
Even the Queen of the Great Below.
I grant you a boon, ask what you will,
I will withhold nothing from you.

Great Queen, we ask only for Inanna, your sister.
We would return Her to Heaven, if you allow.
I do. She now understands sorrow and death.
You may take Her with you, and also my blessing.

I have passed through death and returned to the light,
Thank you, my sister, for showing the way.
Inanna sits on the Throne of Heaven,
Giving life to all the world . . .

Thank you, my sister, for making your journey,
Which brought me those who eased my heart.
Ereshkigal sits in her lapis hall,
Welcoming the dead souls home . . .

Ereshkigal: Lady of Shadows

BellaDonna Oya

I worked with Ereshkigal for quite some time as a matron deity. Despite her reputation as a scary, horrible goddess, I didn't find her to be that way at all; in fact, most women are drawn to her at some point in life, although they usually don't realize it. Elizabeth Barrette gives her the titles of She Who Complains and Goddess of Thankless Tasks.[1] I feel these are both very apt. As She Who Complains, Ereshkigal is the voice inside of us that says, "Are you going to TAKE that? You don't have to! You need to stand up and say you've had enough!" And when we finally do say "ENOUGH!" it is Ereshkigal's voice we use to make our complaints effective. She is also the matron deity of those who do all the yucky and/or boring but necessary tasks that constantly require someone's attention. Think of cleaning a greasy, dirty oven, doing seemingly endless laundry and grocery shopping, changing diapers, washing dishes, cleaning the toilet and the cat's litter box. How often are you thanked or appreciated for doing these tasks? How often do you feel that what you do is overlooked? Do you see Ereshkigal in your life?

I learned that I could go to her altar and meditate on accepting the tasks I had to do even though I didn't want to. Ereshkigal dealt with many unpleasant things, such as the death of her husband and the insults to her sovereignty, so she understands. I found that by putting representations of those tasks on her altar, I could scream, yell and complain about them, then accept them and let go of the anger. I also learned that I can

---

[1] Barrette, Elizabeth 1997 [1995] "Erishkegal: Goddess of Thankless Tasks." *In* SageWoman, Vol. 31, Autumn 1995. Electronic document, accessed 02/12/2007,
http://www.worthlink.net/~ysabet/spirit/erishkegal.

take my grievances to her, lay them at her feet, and practice how to tell people that I wasn't going to put up with that any more.

To honor Ereshkigal is to honor the difficult things in life that we cannot avoid, but that will make us stronger if we face them. Miriam Harline says in her essay on crone goddesses, "Despair, depression and death can be honored as a gift, and not just in a superficial chirpy way that assumes they can thus be placated and avoided... It's also true that only once we truly honor Ereshkigal can we, like Inanna, get off the hook and return to the upper world."[2] While I'm not sure I can ever consider despair or depression as gifts, I can appreciate that they are valid feelings we all have, and that going through them makes me more appreciative of the good things in my life and helps me to be more understanding when others go through them.

How can we honor this goddess? Easy. We can say "thank you" to people who do the nasty, dirty jobs that need doing in order for us to function in a clean environment. (I ran through the mud in our community garden one year to thank the driver of the sewage truck for keeping our portable toilets so clean, and to wish him a Merry Christmas. He was VERY surprised and pleased!) We can honor her by honoring ourselves and learning to say "no" when people ask us to do more than we can reasonably take on. We can sign petitions, write letters and publicly protest spending money on unnecessary wars and new weapons, and recommend instead that it be put into finding cures for AIDS, cancer and other major diseases. (If we try to lighten Ereshkigal's load of death, she will help us lighten our own loads.) And we can weep with and comfort those who mourn, sharing their sorrow because we are all in this world together. As John Donne said, "No man is an island, entire of itself... Every man's death diminishes me, because I am involved in mankind..." While we will probably never be able to eliminate the need for Ereshkigal's presence in the world, we can bring her out of the House of Dust and give her the acknowledgment and respect she deserves.

---

[2] Harline, Miriam 2006 Crone Visions. Electronic document, accessed 02/15/2007, http://www.widdershins.org/vol3iss5/s9704.htm.

Mourning Prayer to Ereshkigal

Rebecca Buchanan

Nether Queen
Soul Shelter
Who welcomes the dead into your darkness
  your warmth
  your arms
Who weeps for the babe who comes too soon
  the warrior bearing the wounds of battle
  the mother with swollen breasts unsuckled
  the grandfather with hands gnarled and weary
Nether Queen
Soul Shelter
Welcome ___ into your darkness
  your warmth
  your arms

Ereshkigal's Visit

Belladonna Laveau

Ereshkigal and Inanna came to me in the summer of 2004, when I started my book tour.[1] They started teaching me many lessons about balance, about the dance of light and dark, and about appreciating the resistance in the path as much as the blessings. These lessons began to lead to many understandings of how struggle brings growth, and how we learn from suffering. I gained many blessings during that time, and as my ministry grew I said many times that if I ever had an opportunity to do a series of rituals where I could be able to put enough effort into it, I would do a really elaborate "Descent of Inanna". It was not too many years later that the opportunity presented itself, when my coven was booked to do four rituals in a row during the month of October.

I asked a spirit sister of mine, Inara de Luna, who I knew was learning similar lessons, to share this experience with me. She agreed and we began to write the ritual. We decided that we would switch roles halfway through the series. I would do the first two as Ereshkigal, as I was comfortable with her energy and had been through a dark time myself. Then I would do Inanna for the last two. We started at a Pagan Pride day, introducing ourselves to the community, sharing our individual perspectives as Goddesses of the myth, and preparing people for the elaborate rituals that many of them would be participating in as the Fall gathering season developed.

Pagan Pride day went well, and I was excited about the upcoming events. Ereshkigal's lessons brought enlightenment to my soul. I understood how she felt, both in being the sufferer of lessons and as the teacher who brought lessons to others and had to suffer with them. Having recently experienced a period of

---

[1] Awakening Spirit, First Year Certification for Wiccan Clergy, Trafford Publishing, Nov 2004, ISBN: 9781412012294.

burnout, I felt her indifference as well as her determination. Within Ereshkigal, I found an appreciation for the darkness I did not know before.

As the time of the next ritual, the full descent, drew near, I could feel the power building. People began putting together the various gates around the land. Our vision started coming into view, and we were all very excited. Inara and I work well together; we are very much a balance of opposites. We mirror so much of each other, it's easy to envision her as my Sister of Heaven and Earth.

As I prepared myself with Ereshkigal's face, I could feel Her coming to me. I put out all my makeup and let her choose how she wanted to look. I found myself putting white and black on my face in some very extreme, and intense, but darkly beautiful angles and shadows. As I became her, I felt frustrated, isolated, alone, misunderstood. I noticed my attendant wasn't attending me. I drove to the drum circle alone, with everyone else in a rush to get ritual ready. There were many details, many gates. I did not care. I was centered within myself, focused on my own needs. I prepared the music. It was about the depravity of mankind, to a very funky beat. I hoped it would be a nice irony of entertainment within the dreadful message of drug abuse, suicide, and several other horrible paths that lead to Ereshkigal. I was cold.

My throne room was the drum circle. It was October, and the temperature had dropped fast. There was a fire in front of me, but it was too far away to warm me. There were torches lighting the circumference of my area and torches that lit either side of my throne, yet the darkness was tangible. For the others, the journey started at the top of the hill, a couple of hundred yards away at the main ritual circle. Rather than finding the usual circle of friends waiting for them, each person who entered the circle found a gateway to the underworld and began their descent through the gates to the lower circle, where I waited.

"I *had* an attendant!" I thought, exasperated that I was left to care for all my own details, all made up dripping with clothing, and jewelry. I could hardly find my hands, much less use them. I noticed he was busy seeing to Inanna. This did not please me. I felt a stab of jealousy, which I felt was inappropriate and pushed away. I climbed up into my throne without assistance, hoping the seat would make me happier.

I waited. . . I was waiting, *forever*! *Is there a problem?* I wondered, frustrated at having to sit in the cold. I sat sullen by a fire that did not warm me, with no one around to ask, in what felt like blackness. I waited, alone, my anger growing. Finally they came. They were cold, and confused. They were expecting something. They looked at me, in my ill temper, as I waited. They sat down, tentatively, they waited with me. Still more came.

How am I going to do a ritual like this? I wondered, agitated and frustrated. *I'm so pissed.* what *is taking so long! Who is not considering how long these people are waiting? *I* am waiting?!?* I was practically screaming in my head.

We waited in the dark and the cold together, in silence. The music amused me at times. I wondered what they were thinking as they stared at me. The temperature had dropped below freezing. *Why do we always think it's a good idea to invoke the Underworld?* I thought to myself, *It never ceases to drop below freezing just as soon as you do that.* The complaining in my head became almost more than I could take, and I was about to call my attendant to me and ask W.T.F.?!?

And then She came. . . Inanna. She would demand and dare to yell at Me? She had been stripped of all her queenly finery and stood in front of me cold and naked. Frustrated and confused herself, her long blond hair her only protection, She demanded to learn the mysteries of death. I thought to myself, "She does not know the consequences of what she asks." So cold, I felt My hand close around My sword. I stood and screamed. It was the loudest scream I had ever heard. It came from deep within Me. It came with pain, and suffering, anger and confusion. It was a scream of torment and outrage. I watched Inanna fall dead in front of Me, and saw them drag Her body away. But I was not concerned with Her.

My attention instead turned to those who would call themselves children of the dark, the hidden children of the Goddess, those who would walk in My realm. They come to Me seeking safety and refuge from the pains of life. They do *not* find it. Like Inanna, they come to my realm dressed in fancy clothing, dripping with crystals and magical tools, a drum and cape in tow,

hoping to learn the mysteries of magic. Yet I clearly warn them...
My priestesses clearly warn them... These are the mysteries of
Death and Initiation. Death... Do you really wish to know?

Dragging my sword in the sand behind me, tired and
frustrated, I cried out to them. I wanted them to understand that
they receive what they ask for. Change and Death are one in the
same. I heard Her speak through me. She said...

*The ways of the Underworld are not your ways. The ways
of the Underworld are my ways. They are perfect and are
not to be questioned ... Yet question them you do.*

*I take the time to mold you, and define you, to guide
you, and teach you. My face is who you see when there is
nothing left. When there is change, transformation, deep
knowing and understanding, you will find Me. When you
are alone, I am there with you. You may dance in the sun of
Inanna all you like, revel in Her pleasures. But if you seek
to know Me, look within the suffering of your soul. You
agree to suffer to learn, and yet you wish to suffer not. You
run away from that which scares you, and rail against the
pain of the path. Yet when the path blooms beneath your
feet, you do not grow stronger. It is only when I am pushing
against you that your muscles are strengthened. Yet you
rage against me when I take the time to do it.*

*If your path be laden with roses, and you struggle not,
then know truly: you are not accomplishing much. Know
that when your heart is rending, when your brain is
reeling, when your world is spinning, that you will learn
how to balance this, and for it you will be better. Know that
the challenges you find are those that I place upon your
path, and be grateful for my ministering. Know that I
prepare you for greater challenges to come.*

*Anyone can rest on laurels and laugh the day away. It
takes an ambitious soul to desire to know the mysteries of
my realm. Know that your desire for this knowledge, set
your feet upon this path before you were born. This
contract you made with me prior to this incarnation. Call
me by what name you will. I am the Dark Goddess, the
Mother of Witches; She who teaches the powers of change.*

I allow you access or not. I give you guidance or My many attendants send you back to the surface, unaware that you never made it to My chamber door.

I have laid your path out before you in the stars, that you may achieve your goals, and walk it you will. Yet you will not walk it alone. I am with you with every step you take. You and I have work to do together, you belong to Me, and I to you: you who would work magic and know the ways of the Underworld. Know then, that your ways were left behind when you stepped into the darkness. The ways of the Underworld are my ways, you will get what you need, in perfect time as the path unfolds.

My ways are perfect. Rage not against your lessons. Know that you are only stepping up to greater challenges as your abilities grow, and be thankful for the opportunity. Death is the doorway that leads to rebirth. I am the Goddess of Life and Death. Death and Life. You cannot be delivered without first letting go.

Let go with grace.

Inanna was then revived and returned to Her kingdom, renewed and better for her visit. The participants came and spoke to Ereshkigal and Inanna in their shrines. Ereshkigal helped many see how their struggles had made them who they are today, and helped them transform their pain into understanding.

I left ritual feeling great. My students took down the ritual areas and grounded. I felt very clear and focused as I made my way back to the campsite, undressed, and got things ready for bed. It was cold, so I stoked a fire in the center of my hand sewn, 18 ft. tipi, my second home. Our native tent heated up nicely and I readied the beds for my three children to come in later and snuggle in for the evening. My lover, Dusty, asked me if I wanted a drink; I refused. I was drinking water, and planned to be very responsible with my energy for the evening.

I did not remove Her face. I did not take the skulls from my hair. I did not formally devoke. I felt good, and didn't want to. I refused food and headed back down to the gathering to spend time with my loved ones in the after ritual glow.

As I walked through the Great Hall, hugging my friends and loved ones, I checked on my kids and then walked out the back of the Hall to where the ritual staff was gathering. Suddenly Daniel, my summoner, grabbed me and shook me, screaming in my face, "Bella, THE TIPI IS ON FIRE!" Stunned, I looked up the hill and indeed saw a screaming skirted Goddess roaring into the air. I shook my head, and thought *This can't be happening, delete, rewind, this isn't real.* I took off at a run back up the hill.

My heart was pounding; I could not move fast enough. I thanked Goddess my children were still safely in the Great Hall behind me, as I watched the men moving vehicles away to safety. I saw Dusty moving my car. There was nothing else on fire. No other tents were harmed. But the canvas of the tipi went very quickly, then the frame and all within. Everything I had for the gathering was ruined: years of clothes, ritual gear, blankets, beds, everything. I stood there, in Ereshkigal's face, as the words that she spoke to others that evening echoed in my ears.

The community came to put out the fire and offer emergency supplies for the evening. They hugged me and told me, "It's what you said, Bella. It's exactly what you said."

"I know!" I cried in return. And I did know. No one was hurt. Most of my belongings had been left at home because I was in a hurry to leave and so did not bring several boxes. I had complained all weekend about the absence of my skirts and various supplies, not realizing that it was all part of the design. I did not lose anything I wasn't meant to lose.

The next day we went through the rubble. We found a whole package of incense that did not burn. We found melted and wet messes of plastic and metals that were useless. We found some tarot cards that did not burn, only three, with interesting messages upon each.

"Master your thoughts"

"If you determine your course with force or speed, you miss the way of the law"

"Even in the empty forest, he finds joy because he wants nothing"

Then we found something that was not a part of my tent, something that I did not bring with me, nor would be likely to have around. I'm not much of a card-giving person. If you get a gift from me, rarely will a card be attached. I don't buy them, and I rarely keep them if they are given to me. So there is no way I would have a random, unsigned card laying around my home, much less my campsite. Yet a greeting card is what we found.

The margin was burned, but the outside read "Our Friendship is Special to Me." Inside it said, "There are friends I can laugh with, or share happy times with, enjoying whatever we do. There are friends I can even share secrets or dreams with, but no friend is closer than you!" The card was unsigned, but the burned out space of the margin looked like the outline of Ereshkigal's throne.

I cried, I accepted the loss, and I let it go. People asked me if I was going to rebuild. I want another tipi, but no. I filed an insurance claim on the loss and ended up better off than when I started. I cannot say I have never railed against the path since then, but I can say that every time a challenge presents itself, I smile and ask "Mom" what the heck I'm supposed to be learning from *this* one. And I never feel like I'm doing it alone now.

Inara and I did the other two rituals. I invoked Inanna the next time, and Inara was Ereshkigal. She received her lessons and we decided to end the rituals in the roles we both found most comfortable: me as the dark Goddess, she as the light. Yet neither of those rituals touched me like the evening the Goddess visited me at my tipi, and left a calling card with her signature on it.

The Dark Mother's Mysteries & Lessons

Inara de Luna

So, I had this great idea: I wanted to enact the Descent of Inanna. I'd been studying this Sumerian Goddess as part of my sacred sexuality studies and had become incredibly intrigued by her journey to the Underworld. In a serendipitous conversation with my good friend and fellow priestess, Bella, we discovered that we both had a desire to create this ritual for a large group. We decided to devote the whole month of October 2007, to this project. We had four events, one every weekend that month, to take four different groups through the descent. We decided further that it would be great if we switched off the two main parts: she would invoke Ereshkigal for the first two, while I invoked Inanna; then we would switch places for the last two events. This way, we thought, we would both get to experience both sides of this working.

I loved being Inanna — the bright Goddess of Heaven and Earth, the embodiment of beauty, grace, power, and sexual independence. She inhabited me as if she belonged, and I thoroughly enjoyed every moment. However, I didn't learn as much from her as I did from her Dark Sister.

The first time we did this ritual was during our local Pagan Pride day, where Bella and I circled one another, invoked as Ereshkigal and Inanna, respectively, and we described who and what we were.

Ereshkigal: *I am Ereshkigal, the Dark Mother, Queen of the Dead. I am the Queen of all Witches. You come to me to learn the mysteries of intuition, magic, and sorcery. You come to me when the moon is full, and ask of me to deliver my deepest secrets, and I give them to you. All acts of pain and suffering are my tests.*

Inanna: *I am Inanna, the Bright Mother, Queen of Heaven and Earth. Mine is the ecstasy of the spirit and mine also is joy on earth.*

My law is love unto all beings. You come to me in worship, and dance in my honor. You revel in my blessings. All acts of love and pleasure are my rituals.

We were mostly talking to the crowd, I carrying a beautiful staff crowned with white and silver, while she carried a large, intimidating sword. Our lines gradually moved into veiled insults of one another.

Inanna: *I am the beauty of the green earth, and the desire in the heart of man. I come to you in the face of your loved ones, your mother's soft touch, your father's gentle security, your best friend's support, and your lover's caress. I have created all this beauty for you to enjoy. I ensure that you never have lack, that you are always comforted, and safe. From me, all things proceed.*

Ereshkigal: *And unto me,* all things must return. *I ensure that you do lack, and that you are sometimes uncomfortable. Without these struggles, you would be a spoiled and soft people, easily misled, easily lied to, easily conquered. Is this what you want? Do you want to be coddled and safe? Provided for? Like puppies? I come to you in the face of your loved ones, and your enemies. You will see my dark and terrible face reflected back by those who challenge you, who oppose you, who cause you to rethink, overcome, and prevail. You dishonor me when you hate and rage against the mysteries only I can bring. You dishonor the path when you hate and rage against your brothers and sisters.*

Finally Bella/Ereshkigal rushed at me with her sword aimed at my head. I raised my staff and blocked her blow and we locked eyes. This intense moment was a challenge: the Dark Sister daring Her light half to brave Her dark realm and experience what it really meant to learn the dark mysteries.

The following weekend, we were at a full weekend festival out in the wilds of west Georgia. We each dressed in our ritual outfits, applied our make-up and did our hair and then we split up: she was off to the drum circle, which was to serve as her Underworld domain, to await the souls who chose to make the journey. Meanwhile, I wandered the entire festival grounds, proclaiming to all my intentions to confront my Sister in her realm:

I go to the Underworld, the realm of my sister, Queen Ereshkigal. I go to learn from her the mysteries of the Underworld, so that I may find a way to bring relief to my people. I have attired myself with all the symbols of my station and authority, as befits a Queen, for I am Inanna, Goddess of Heaven and Earth! If you choose to accompany me down the dark path to the Underworld, please equip yourself with all that you are, that you may be prepared for this journey.

Finally, we arrived at the top of the hill that represented the first of seven gates to be passed through on the way to Ereshkigal's realm. At each gate was stationed a guardian who challenged every one of us, and as the last to pass through each gate, I, as Inanna, was required to remove some piece of jewelry or part of my garment before passage was granted. I eventually arrived at the final gate, whereupon I was required to remove my final garment; I entered the Underworld completely naked. Holding my head high, trying to maintain my queenly dignity even while nude and stripped of all my articles of power, I stalked toward Ereshkigal where she sat arrogantly upon her throne. Immediately, I started making demands, very aware of the responsibility my people had placed on me to alleviate the hardships they endured in their lives.

She looked me dead in the eye, stood slowly and imperiously, and uttered a deathly scream. I was struck down, the power of her voice robbing me of life. I crumpled to the ground before her throne and was dragged off to the side by her minions while she addressed the crowd of souls that had dared the same journey.

Eventually, I was revived by the water and bread of life brought by Enki's little genderless beings, whereupon I stood to face my sister and apologized for my own arrogance and lack of understanding. We embraced, and then stood upon our own shrines to minister individually to the people who had attended the ritual. Many hugs and tears and expressions of gratitude were exchanged. Finally, we closed the ritual, but we were so giddy that the ritual had been so successful, and so eager to get to the party planned for afterward, that we neglected to formally devoke.

About half an hour into the party, we heard yells coming from the area of the festival grounds where Bella was camped. "Bella's tipi is on fire!" And sure enough, when we looked up the hill, a huge blaze was roaring! Everyone went running: some up to the tipi itself, some to the kitchen with buckets, bowls, trash cans, and anything else we could think of in which to carry water. We were desperate to get the fire out before it could spread to the trees or any other tents. An amazingly hot fire, it quickly destroyed the entire tipi and most of its contents, mostly personal items belonging to Bella and her family. Thank the Goddess, no one was seriously hurt. Her children had not been in or near the tipi when it caught, and the only injury I heard of was a volunteer that got hit in the head by one of the tipi poles when it fell.

When the fire was finally out and the excitement had died down, I crumpled into a heap. Watching Bella's tipi burn down after she wore Ereshkigal's face and knowing that I would then be playing that role the very next weekend terrified me. Not only was I personally afraid of losing something as a direct result of invoking Her energy, I was also confronted with a dramatic example of the power and responsibility we have as magical people. Part of me wanted to run away, to forget that magic even existed, to stop "playing the game." But, as She conveyed, there is no turning back. You can't unlearn what you've learned, not and live authentically.

It became apparent to me that this whole experience was giving me the opportunity to dive even more deeply into magical understanding of myself and the world; to communicate more often and more succinctly with the Gods; to honor the responsibility I have been given.

So, after much intense soul searching during the following week, I went ahead and bravely invoked Ereshkigal myself. I remember as I began to dress, do my hair, and especially as I started to apply my make-up, that with each action I was invoking Her more and more. This particular deific energy was unlike anything I'd ever felt before. It was heavy and dark, and full of anger, sadness, and other "negative" emotions. I found that my easy smile was nowhere to be found. My partner asked me if I was okay, and I assured him that nothing was wrong personally, but that the Goddess was already riding me hard.

We were finally ready to begin, and so I made my way to the drum circle/throne room and climbed atop my throne. I watched as the little people hesitantly stepped into my realm; I nodded regally at those brave enough to acknowledge me. I was still and quiet, awaiting my sister, knowing I would soon kill her, and feeling a strange sort of triumphant sadness in the knowledge. Finally, she arrived, and flounced before me in all her splendid nude beauty. I was suddenly enraged by her, by all of what she represented, by the neglect I had suffered from both the other gods and by the humans in her realm. I couldn't even hear what she was saying; I just stood up, opened my mouth and screamed. Even now, remembering back on this moment, the hair stands up on my arms and a chill runs down the back of my neck.

She crumpled at my feet and I waved at my minions to move her worthless corpse from my sight. I stood and climbed down from my throne, clutching my blade, and I surveyed the cowering humans before me. They had been shivering and complaining of the cold and I was incensed. How dare they come down to my realm, of their own free will, and complain about something so insignificant as the cold? I then asked them to remember some of my harsher lessons and explained that if their lives were always soft and safe and comfortable, they would never grow. As harsh as my lessons may be, they come from my desire to make a person strong and beautiful, like a sword, which must be thrust into the fire and pounded repeatedly before it emerges as a useful tool of beauty.

I mourned the lack of appreciation or acknowledgement I generally receive for my efforts. I lamented the pain I endure. I cried out against my loneliness. I gradually realized that these two strange little beings were empathizing with me. Finally, someone was hearing and validating me! And they had compassion for me! I cried out in relief and offered them anything in my power to give, to thank them for that tiny, but hugely significant gift. All they wanted was Inanna's corpse, which I had no use for, so they revived her. Once reanimated, she came and stood before me, and expressed her sorrow for not understanding and her gratitude for my lessons. I finally felt heard and seen by my sister of the Light, and felt hope that her followers would better appreciate my role in their lives. We embraced, then parted to receive the humans who remained and would soon be returning to their world. Many tears and laughter and hugs were shared. This time, after the people had dispersed, a priest approached us individually and formally and thoroughly thanked and devoked the Goddess' presences from us, and we each made an offering to the fire. Fortunately, we had learned our lesson and nothing needed to be sacrificed this time.

The following weekend, the fourth and final in our series, Bella and I reverted back to our original roles: I would wear Inanna's face again, while Bella was ridden by Ereshkigal. We both decided that we were far more comfortable in these roles, and that we had learned the lessons we needed from the opposite. Our last re-enactment of this ritual theater went off splendidly, and nothing burned down that time, either. Our divine commitment was complete.

* * * * * * * * * * * * *

Invoking Ereshkigal was a difficult thing for me. Inanna is a far more natural fit, and so learning to become Ereshkigal was quite a stretch. But it taught me a lot. Not only do I more deeply understand Her lessons associated with loss and hardship and that it all happens for a reason, namely to make us stronger, but now I also understand how Her role as the Goddess of Thankless Tasks translates to my role as a priestess, teacher and leader in the community. Sometimes I will have to convey a hard truth to someone who may not want to hear it. Sometimes I may have to tell someone "No." I may not always be liked and appreciated, and that has to be okay.

Ereshkigal helped me to more deeply understand the importance of death in the cycle. And not just physical death, but symbolic death. We must die in order to be reborn, both within this life and in the greater cycle. With each personal transformation, a part of us dies and must be let go, in order to complete the transformation.

Finally, I was also needing balance. I seek the Light, the Love, the Joy, the Compassion . . . and sometimes I neglect the darker, shadowy aspects of myself and of life in general. Wearing Ereshkigal's face was a heavy burden and it was not fun. I felt deeper anger, sorrow and frustration than I normally do. Her rage filled me up and She required me to be direct and confrontational — an interpersonal style that I am neither accustomed to nor comfortable with. When I/Ereshkigal asked Bella/Inanna if she was willing to embrace her Shadow/Sister, I was really asking that question of myself. And I can now say, after completing this series of rituals, that I am, and that I am prepared to accept responsibility for my dark half, in a way that I couldn't even comprehend before.

Queen Ereshkigal, I offer this to you as a sign of my understanding and acceptance. Please accept this offering in the spirit in which it is given. Thank you for the opportunity to learn your lessons and to convey them to the community. Thank you for all that I have endured to reach this place, which enabled me to carry this off. I honor you.

Ereshkigal Speaks

Belladonna Laveau & Inara de Luna

These words were spoken by the priestesses channeling the Goddess Ereshkigal during the Descent of Inanna re-enactment in October 2007. Bella and Inara took turns throughout the month playing the characters of the two goddesses, and these words were divinely inspired.

I am Ereshkigal, the Dark Mother, Goddess of the Dead. I am the Queen of all Witches. I am not often given voice. But now that you have called to me, I have much to say.

You come to me to learn the mysteries of intuition, magic, and sorcery. You seek to know the great mysteries hidden in the stars, you ask me to teach you the secrets of my realm. You come to me when the moon is full, and ask of me to deliver my deepest secrets, and I give them to you. But then you run from me in fear and spit your anger back at me. You do not want to pay my price. Even now with all that you have learned, and all that you have gained, you long for what you have given up. All acts of pain and suffering are my tests.

How do you trust that which scares you?

Mine is the Cauldron of Cerridwen, which is the Holy Grail of Immortality. You beg for my help. But then you cry and wail against me, for taking away what no longer serves you. You shrink from the challenges I bring before you. But once you step upon my spiraling path, there is no turning back. You cannot undo the vows you make to me; you cannot unlearn my mysteries. And yes... they do hurt. They leave marks upon your soul.

Every single one of you has experienced loss and hardship and you have learned from that experience. But you don't often give thanks for that experience. You don't trust me. You don't believe that I love you. And so the lesson goes unheeded. You fear me, as you should. But you also forget me, you intentionally close your ears to me, and you don't thank me. When you do this, you don't incorporate my lessons and so I have to hit you again and again and again, harder each time.

Tell me, what gifts of pain and suffering have I given you? What hurts do you harbor in your heart?

I am not nice, but I am not here to punish you. I am harsh, but I am not vindictive. You start as shapeless, formless, useless blobs, and that's how you would stay if it weren't for me. I thrust you into the fire and pound you over and over, until you have become strong and beautiful. Like my sword.

I challenge you to succeed. Through my mysteries you will not be vulnerable and naive, easily defeated, easily controlled. Is this *not* love?

Yes, I will burn your shit down! If that is what you need. Remember, my ways are perfect, but they are not your ways. Everything you experience happens for a reason, but you may not immediately be able to see or understand that reason. And that's why you need to trust me. Even when you're scared shitless.

My lessons are not easy, or fun, or pleasurable – but they help you to appreciate all the wonderful things in your life. And they bring you together in ways that comfort and pleasure cannot.

I ensure that you *do* lack, and that you are sometimes uncomfortable. Can you face your fears and walk the path with honor and respect for those who teach you lessons, both good and horrible? I come to you in the face of your loved ones and your enemies. You will see my dark and terrible face reflected back by those who challenge you, who oppose you, who cause you to rethink, overcome, and prevail.

Yet my wisdom lies deep within you. It comes from within, and so you think it's you. You think *you* taught yourself this all on your own. You are an arrogant one! You do not appreciate the gifts I give you. My temples are barren and in need of repair. I receive no offerings for ministering to you. My priests and priestesses are scorned, for the lessons they have taught brought you pain and suffering. You do not honor me. You are not grateful for my gifts.

So many paths entwine as one. So much work that must be done. You cannot see the cloth as it weaves. You cannot see when the thread is complete. You do not know all the others you affect. You do not consider the lives you may wreck.

Are your goals and desires, and hopes and good deeds, still important to you in the face of others' needs?

How often do you call on the gods? How often do you ask for their assistance? How often do you express thanks to the gods and serve them or their people? Remember, you must sometimes give before you can get. The gods need thanks and appreciation, to be honored and served. Don't forget to acknowledge the gifts they've already given you. We are all born with gifts and it closes us off to further blessings when we take these gifts for granted or don't utilize them. Sometimes, sacrifice is required. Sometimes, surrender. You must be prepared to give up all that you have, all that you are, in order to transform into all that you might become. You must be prepared to submit and surrender to the will of the gods, even when it hurts, if you truly wish to embrace all the gifts they have for you.

The Ways of the Underworld

Janet Munin

I.

Ereshkigal went her way in the Great Below.
In the dark regions below the earth, Ereshkigal the Queen went
  her way.
The realm of Irkalla was in order.
There was peace in the Great Below.
All things were as they should be.

The silence of the underworld was broken by a crash.
The peace of the Great Below was shattered by someone
  pounding on the gates.

Ereshkigal called out to her steward Neti:
"Who batters on the gate of the Great Below?
Who violates the peace of Irkalla?
Who demands entry where no creature seeks to go?"

Neti was obedient to the command of his queen.
The steward rose to the gates of Irkalla and returned.

"My queen, Inanna your sister demands entry to your realm.
The Evening Star seeks to descend to the Great Below.
Inanna comes to the gate of the underworld with all her powers
  gathered around her.

Inanna has put on the crown of the steppes.
She has tied strings of small lapis beads around her neck.
A double strand of beads falls over her chest.
Inanna wears the breastplate called *Come Man Come*.
On her wrist is a gold bracelet, and the lapis measuring rod and
  line are in her hand.
Inanna has put on the robe of royalty."

Ereshkigal smote her thigh in rage.
The Queen of the Great Below shrieked in anger.
She cried out, "My sister's passions know no bounds!
Inanna's desires know no law.
The Evening Star has never kept her course!

The Great Above is hers.
The making of kings is hers.
The keeping of the <u>mes</u> is hers,
But she is not content.
My sister will not be satisfied.

Inanna hungers for the Great Below,
But the Great Below will consume her.
The laws of Irkalla will prevail even over the will of the Evening
  Star."

Ereshkigal said to Neti, "Let Inanna enter.
Let my sister pass into my realm.
But at each gate take from her an emblem of her power.
Let the Evening Star be cast down!"

Neti departed.
The steward of Irkalla went to do the bidding of his queen.

Ereshkigal walked around her throne room.
The Queen of the Great Below moved silently in the shadows.
The dust of the underworld bore the marks of her passing.

Far above, Inanna reached the first gate of the underworld.
As she passed through, the crown of the steppes was taken from
  her head.

"What is this?" Inanna protested.

Ereshkigal stood still.
Through the mouth of the gatekeeper she rebuked her sister.
"Be silent, Inanna! The ways of the underworld are perfect.
O Inanna, do not question the ways of the underworld."

The Queen of Heaven gnashed her teeth in rage.
Heaven held its breath.
Earth held its breath.
The Great Below watched silently, and waited.
Inanna walked on.

Ereshkigal walked a second time around her throne room.

Inanna reached the second gate of the underworld.
As she passed through, the strands of small lapis beads were
  taken from her neck.

"What is this?" Inanna cried.

Through the mouth of the gatekeeper Ereshkigal rebuked her
  sister.
"Be silent, Inanna! The ways of the underworld are perfect.
O Inanna, do not question the ways of the underworld."

The Queen of Heaven clutched her throat.
Heaven held its breath.
Earth held its breath.
The Great Below watched silently, and waited.
Inanna walked on.

Ereshkigal walked a third time around her throne room.

Inanna reached the third gate of the underworld.
As she passed through, the double strand of beads was taken
  from her chest.

"What is this?" Inanna shrieked.

Through the mouth of the gatekeeper Ereshkigal rebuked her
  sister.
"Be silent, Inanna! The ways of the underworld are perfect.
O Inanna, do not question the ways of the underworld."

The Queen of Heaven pressed her hands to her chest.
Heaven held its breath.

Earth held its breath.
The Great Below watched silently, and waited.
Inanna walked on.

Ereshkigal walked a fourth time around her throne room.

Inanna reached the fourth gate of the underworld.
As she passed through, the breastplate called *Come, Man, Come*
was taken from her.

"What is this?" Inanna demanded.

Through the mouth of the gatekeeper Ereshkigal rebuked her
sister.
"Be silent, Inanna! The ways of the underworld are perfect.
O Inanna, do not question the ways of the underworld."

The Queen of Heaven clutched at her breasts.
Heaven held its breath.
Earth held its breath.
The Great Below watched silently, and waited.
Inanna walked on.

Ereshkigal walked a fifth time around her throne room.

Inanna reached the fifth gate of the underworld.
As she passed through, her gold bracelet was taken from her.

"What is this?" Inanna groaned.

Through the mouth of the gatekeeper Ereshkigal rebuked her
sister.
"Be silent, Inanna! The ways of the underworld are perfect.
O Inanna, do not question the ways of the underworld."

The Queen of Heaven grasped at her wrist.
Heaven held its breath.
Earth held its breath.
The Great Below watched silently, and waited.
Inanna walked on.

Ereshkigal walked a sixth time around her throne room.

Inanna reached the sixth gate of the underworld.
As she passed through, her lapis rod and measuring line were
  taken from her.

"What is this?" Inanna moaned.

Through the mouth of the gatekeeper Ereshkigal rebuked her
  sister.
"Be silent, Inanna! The ways of the underworld are perfect.
O Inanna, do not question the ways of the underworld."

The Queen of Heaven wrung her empty hands.
Heaven held its breath.
Earth held its breath.
The Great Below watched silently, and waited.
Inanna walked on.

Ereshkigal walked a seventh time around her throne room.

Inanna reached the seventh gate of the underworld.
As she passed through, her royal robe was taken from her.

"What is this?" Inanna whispered.

Through the mouth of the gatekeeper Ereshkigal rebuked her
  sister.
"Be silent, Inanna! The ways of the underworld are perfect.
O Inanna, do not question the ways of the underworld."

Inanna swayed in horror.
The Queen of Heaven shivered in her nakedness.
Heaven held its breath.
Earth held its breath.
The Great Below watched silently, and waited.
Inanna stumbled on.

The Queen of the Great Below seated herself on her lapis throne.
The Annunaki gathered around her.

Inanna entered the throne room naked and bowed low.
The Queen of Heaven bent down before the throne of Irkalla.

Inanna stretched out her hand to Ereshkigal.
Words of entreaty choked her throat like dust.
Ereshkigal rose from her throne.
The Queen of the Great Below spoke the word of wrath against
    Inanna.
Ereshkigal smote Inanna with the eye of death.

The Queen of Heaven was no more.

The Evening Star was turned into a slab of rotting meat.
Ereshkigal hung the meat on a hook in her throne room.

"The ways of the underworld are perfect," she whispered.
"O rotting meat, do not question the ways of the underworld."

Three days passed.

II.

Ereshkigal the Queen sat on her throne in the underworld.
Ereshkigal moaned with pain like a woman in childbirth.
The Queen of the Great Below moaned like a new mother in her
    labor.

Above, in the city of Nippur, Ninshubur entreated the great god
    Enlil:
"Do not let Inanna die in the underworld!"
But Enlil would not help.

Ereshkigal mourned the death of Gugalanna, her husband.
The Queen of the Great Below wept for the Great Bull of Heaven.
Ereshkigal raged for the loss of her husband.

"For Inanna you died!" she cried.
"To defend the honor of my sister you did battle with Gilgamesh
    and were overthrown.

For Inanna's sake were you killed,
And your corpse was desecrated by Enkidu!
The Great Bull of Heaven will come no more to my bed.
My husband will no longer hold me in the dark nights of Irkalla!"

Ereshkigal clutched her belly like a woman in the pains of labor.

Above, in the city of Ur, Ninshubur entreated the moon god Nanna:
"Do not let Inanna die in the underworld!"
But Nanna would not help.

Ereshkigal raged at the corpse of Inanna.
She cursed the rotting meat that hung in the throne room.

"Inanna, the Great Above was yours!
O my sister, the holy <u>mes</u> were yours!
Inanna, the making of kings was yours!
The plenty of the storehouse was yours!
The beads of the harlot were yours!
The inspiring of lust was yours!

Inanna, you wandered to and fro in the streets of heaven and
   earth
while I remained in the Great Below.
Inanna, you were loved by all the gods and men
while I am feared.
Inanna, you had everything!
Why did you set your ear to the Great Below?
O my sister, why did you seek my portion to add to your own?

Inanna, why did you not leave my husband in peace?
O my sister, why did you not leave my realm in peace?"

Ereshkigal rocked on her throne, crying like a woman giving
   birth.
The Queen of the Great Below wept alone in the shadows of her
   throne room.

Above, in the city of Eridu, Ninshubur entreated Father Enki:
"Do not let Inanna die in the underworld!" – and Father Enki cried,

"The Queen of Heaven must not perish in the Great Below!
Inanna must return to the earth.
Without Inanna, the woman will not turn to the man
The cow will not receive the bull.
Without Inanna, the grains will not rise.
The storehouse will be empty
The people will die!
Inanna must return to the Great Above!"

Father Enki took dirt from beneath his fingernails and created two
sexless beings, the kurgarra and the galatur. He sent them down to
the underworld. Like flies, they slipped through the cracks in the
seven walls of the underworld. They did not arouse the
gatekeepers.

The kurgarra and the galatur found Ereshkigal weeping on her
throne.

"Oh, my husband!" Ereshkigal cried.
"Oh, your husband!" they cried.
"Oh, my sister!" Ereshkigal shrieked.
"Oh, your sister!" they shrieked.
"Oh, my heart!" Ereshkigal sobbed.
"Oh, your heart!" they sobbed.

Ereshkigal raised her head.
The widow of Gugalanna gazed in wonder at the strangers before
  her.

"Who are you who moan and cry with me?
Who are you whose pity eases my heart?
Whoever you are, you will be blessed.
Whatever you wish, it shall be yours."

The *kurgarra* and *galatur* bowed.
"We wish only for the corpse of Inanna."

Ereshkigal realized that they had been sent from Above.
The Queen of Irkalla understood that their sympathy had been
  for her sister's cause.

"Take it," she said – and turned her back on them.

The *kurgarra* and *galatur* took Inanna's corpse from the peg.
They laid the green and stinking meat on the floor of the throne
  room.
They fed Inanna the food and water of life.
The Queen of Heaven rose, radiant in the shadows.
The Evening Star glowed in the darkness of the underworld.

Inanna cried out in triumph:
"The bread of life is mine!
The water of life is mine!
The favor of Father Enki is mine!
O my sister, you cannot defeat me!"

Ereshkigal turned to face her sister.
The Queen of Irkalla gazed on the Holy Priestess of Heaven.
"The ways of the underworld are perfect, my sister.
O Inanna, if you leave Irkalla another must take your place."

"It shall not be!" Inanna replied.
"O my sister, you cannot command such things."

Inanna turned to ascend to the Great Above.
The *galla* demons swarmed in her footsteps.
The Evening Star rose again with the shadow of the underworld
  behind her.

III.

The Queen of Heaven emerged from the underworld.
She found Ninshubur dressed in sackcloth and ashes.
Ninshubur ran to Inanna and knelt, weeping with joy at seeing
  her mistress again.
Inanna raised her and embraced her.

"Give Ninshubur to us!" the *galla* cried – but Inanna refused, for
  she loved her devoted servant.

"Walk on, my sister, walk on," Ereshkigal whispered.

Inanna walked along the road, Ninshubur by her side, the *galla* following behind.
She found Sharra, her son who tended her holy temple. His eyes were red with weeping for his mother's death.
Sharra ran to Inanna and knelt, his tears falling again in joy.
Inanna raised her son and embraced him.

"Give Sharra to us!" the *galla* cried – but Inanna refused, for she loved her loyal son.

"Walk on, my sister, walk on," Ereshkigal whispered.

Inanna continued along the road, Ninshubur by her side, the *galla* following behind.
She found Lulal, her second son, who had rent his clothing in grief for his mother.
Lulal ran to Inanna and knelt before her, crying thanks to the gods for the restoration of his mother.
Inanna raised her son and embraced him.

"Give Lulal to us!" the *galla* cried – but Inanna refused, for she loved her faithful son.

"Walk on, my sister, walk on," Ereshkigal whispered.

Inanna entered her city of Uruk, Ninshubur by her side, the *galla* following behind.
Inanna, the young wife, longed to see her husband Dumuzi again.
Inanna searched the palace for her shepherd king.
Inanna searched the streets for her beloved husband.

She found Dumuzi sitting on a throne under an apple tree.
Inanna found her husband drinking beer and playing on his pipe.
She found her husband enjoying the pleasures of life.

Inanna fixed Dumuzi with the eye of death.
"Take him!" she screamed.

The *galla* threw Dumuzi from his throne.
They bound the shepherd with strong ropes.
They did not listen to his pleas for mercy.
They did not heed his tears.

The Queen of Heaven did not listen to his pleas for mercy.
The Holy Priestess of Heaven did not heed his tears.

The *galla* dragged Dumuzi down to the Great Below.
The *galla* threw the shepherd in the dust at the foot of the
throne.
The husband of Inanna wept and begged for mercy.

Ereshkigal smiled down on him.
"By the word of wrath you have been condemned.
By the eye of death you have been slain.
For Inanna's sake you are consigned to Irkalla.
There is no mercy for you here."

In the dust of the Great Below, Dumuzi wept.
Among the stars in the Great Above, Inanna wept.
In the shadows of Irkalla, Ereshkigal the Queen went her way.

The ways of the underworld are perfect.
O my people, do not question the ways of the underworld.

Meeting Ereshkigal

Janet Munin

If you feel drawn toward Ereshkigal and want to make contact with her, your best resource is your own intuition and inner wisdom. Sit quietly, clear your mind, place yourself under the protection of the highest form of deity you know (or that of the guardians with whom you usually work) and then address yourself to her. Tell her that you would like to meet with her and ask her to grace you with her presence. You may not feel like you get a response. You may have images or words come up which let you know what she would like you to do in order to prepare for such a meeting. You might be surprised by the vivid immediacy of her response. It will all depend on your individual situation, talents, and needs.

If you do not receive a response, or if you want to set up more formal, focused conditions before attempting to communicate with her, the following elements can help create an appropriate ritual atmosphere:

- A black candle
- Myrrh
- A sharp knife, or other object that feels symbolically appropriate to you
- A black or red altar cloth

You may also wish to make an offering of fresh bread and something good to drink, or something of natural beauty. In my experience, Ereshkigal likes white roses.

Waiting until after dark on a night of the new moon can also be helpful.

Set up your altar, light the candle and incense, set some form of protection[1], and then clear your mind. Close your eyes or use the knife (or other symbol) as a focus for meditation. You can also chant, drum, or use other techniques to help shift your consciousness, if you prefer.

Ask Ereshkigal to make herself known to you, and then listen closely for the response. It may be dramatic, but it also may come in a "still, small voice," images, or feelings. If nothing seems to come to you, try using automatic or off-hand writing to allow the goddess to speak through your own shadow-self.

Ereshkigal may make herself present, or you may receive a vision of a downward path or the entrance to a cave and an invitation to descend. Understand that an invitation to descend will not necessarily involve an ordeal, but you may be asked to give one or more items to gatekeepers. You are always free to turn back at any time.

If you do get a response, please exercise basic spiritual common sense and test anything you receive before acting on it. Ereshkigal herself will never seek to demean or injure you, nor will she ever ask you to harm another. She will not ask you for your blood. There are spirits who will take advantage of an inexperienced person by pretending to be a deity in order to advance their own agendas, especially a deity who, like Ereshkigal, has been called on for dark purposes in the past. Placing yourself under protection before you begin a ritual will usually be enough to prevent such an incident, but it's always wise to exercise caution. No authentic deity will ever be insulted if you ask for time to think about something they have told you, or if you tell them you need to take time for discernment.

At the end of your encounter, thank the goddess for her presence and blessings and then transition slowly out of meditative space. Eat and drink something to help ground yourself.

---

[1] This can be as simple as saying a prayer asking the protection of a deity, angel, or guardian spirit. You can also visualize yourself in a circle or sphere of light that nothing can pass if it has ill intent or is contrary to your greatest good.

For Further Reading

As this book goes to press there are very few resources available about Ereshkigal. This list includes those which I have found most useful.

ABOUT ERESHKIGAL

Into The Great Below: A Devotional For Inanna And Ereshkigal by Galina Krasskova

Nergal and Ereshkigal: Re-enchanting the Sumerian Underworld by Lishtar
http://www.gatewaystobabylon.com/religion/nergalereshkigal2000.htm

Desire in Death's Realm: Sex, Power and Violence in "Nergal and Ereshkigal" by Neal Walls in *Desire, Discord and Death: Approaches to Ancient Near East Myth*

The Queen of Swords by Judy Grahn

ON THE GODS AND RELIGION OF THE ANCIENT NEAR EAST

In the Wake of the Goddesses: Women, Culture and the Transformation of Pagan Myth by Tikva Frymer-Kensky

Treasures of Darkness: A History of Mesopotamian Religion by Thorkild Jacobsen

SHADOW WORK, THE ORDEAL PATH & BDSM SPIRITUALITY

Tarot Shadow Work: Using the Dark Symbols to Heal by Christine Jette

Sacred Kink: The Eightfold Paths of BDSM and Beyond by Lee Harrington

Dark Moon Rising: Pagan BDSM and the Ordeal Path by Raven Kaldera

Contributors

Lady Belladonna Laveau, HPS, Dean of WiccanSeminary.edu, High Priestess of the Covenant of WISE, Church of Wicca, and author of *Awakening Spirit* has been an initiate of Wicca and a devoted Priestess of Wicca since 1989. Bella is most often recognized for her appearance on ABC-TV's "Wife Swap." She is a talented healer, Reiki Master, ordained minister and teacher of the Wiccan faith, a Navy veteran, and operates the online Wiccan state-recognized college, The Woolston-Steen Theological Seminary, aka WiccanSeminary.edu.

BellaDonna Oya lives in Hayward, CA, where she is the high priestess of a small eclectic Wiccan coven. Her hobbies are gardening, belly dance, crocheting for charities, Renaissance faires, travel, and cats (she has eleven). She has both a BA and an MA in Anthropology, and is fascinated by mummies, ancient Egypt, and researching Goddess worship through time. She has traveled to Ireland, Jamaica, Eleuthera, and Mexico, and hopes someday to visit Crete, Malta, Egypt and Delphi. Currently, she is widening her spiritual horizons by studying the shamanic path.

Callista Evenstar is a priestess and healer who, during daylight hours, is often mistaken for a simple massage therapy instructor. She's an experience junkie, an ambitious slacker, a crazy cat lady and a beadaholic. She lives in Norfolk, Virginia, with her four furkids, ten featherkids and an incredibly patient partner who keeps her grounded and sane, most of the time.

Clare Vaughn is the pen name of an ordained pagan priestess. Co-author of *Pagan Prayer Beads* and *Learning Ritual Magic*, Clare lives in Western Maryland.

Erynn Rowan Laurie is a poet and professional madwoman living by the shores of the Salish Sea. She is the author of *Circle of*

Stones: Journeys and Meditations for Modern Celts and *Ogam: Weaving Word Wisdom*, along with a growing number of poems, essays and articles on Paganism. She is also a contributor to *Warriors and Kin*, a military Pagan blog that is part of the Pagan Newswire Collective. Erynn's webpage, The Preserving Shrine, can be found at http://www.seanet.com/~inisglas.

Galina Krasskova is a free range tribalist Heathen who has been a priest of Odin and Loki for close to fifteen years. Originally ordained in the Fellowship of Isis in 1995, Ms. Krasskova also attended the oldest interfaith seminary in the U.S. – the New Seminary where she was ordained in 2000. She continues as a guest lecturer and mentor at the New Seminary, and is part of a team of ministers for the Interfaith Fellowship in NYC. She is the founder of Urdabrunnr Kindred (NY), a member of Ironwood Kindred (MA), Asatru in Frankfurt (Frankfurt am Main, Germany), the First Kingdom Church of Asphodel (MA), the American Academy of Religion, and the Religious Coalition for Reproductive Choice. Ms. Krasskova currently writes as a columnist for BBI Media's *Witches and Pagans Magazine*, is an official writer for Patheos' pagan blog *Pantheon*, and she has a variety of published books available running the gamut from introductory texts on the Northern Tradition, to runes, prayer, and devotional practices, with more books on the way.

Grace Barker is a devotee of Anubis. She has been studying shamanism for three years and has belonged to her Master Anubis even longer. She can be contacted at graceatthoughts@gmail.com.

H. Jeremiah Lewis is a Greco-Egyptian polytheist author who has had a life-long love affair with the great civilizations of antiquity and their sacred traditions. He serves the gods and his community under the religious name Sannion and has led a number of successful classes, workshops, and large public rituals. When he isn't studying or writing he can often be found out in the wild places with the nymphs. His home is the lovely city of Eugene, Oregon. His website and blog can be found at www.thehouseofvines.com.

Inara de Luna is a Qadishtu priestess of sacred sexuality and the founder of the Temple of the Red Lotus, an organization devoted to the practice and promotion of sacred sexuality. She offers workshops, classes, rituals and private consultations on sex, love, and relationships, especially as those relate to one's spirituality. She has been published in *The Common People Magazine, Atlanta Rising* magazine, *Six Word Memoirs on Love and Heartbreak*, and has been interviewed on several radio shows. Inara believes that transcendence and spiritual evolution occur through integration and wholeness – bridging the gap between the mind, the body, and the spirit: between masculine and feminine energies; and between the light and the dark on all levels of existence. Her website is www.TempleRedLotus.com. She can be contacted via email at info@templeredlotus.com.

Jerzy Chojnowski is the cover artist. His work can be seen at www.firensephir.deviantart.com. You can contact him at Tanatris@gmail.com.

Lee Harrington is an eclectic artist, spiritual and erotic educator, gender radical and award winning published author on human sexuality and spiritual experience. His books include *Sacred Kink: The Eightfold Paths of BDSM and Beyond*, and his writings and photography have appeared in numerous other publications, such as *Dark Moon Rising: Pagan BDSM and the Ordeal Path* and *Spirals & Shards: Pagan Poetry from the Back of the Heart*, including under his previous name, Bridgett Harrington. Learn more at www.PassionAndSoul.com.

Leni Hester is a witch, ritualist and writer from Denver, Colorado.

MasterAmazon: I came out as a Lesbian, a LeatherDyke, into Goddess Worship as a Witch, and earned my Black Belt in Tae Kwon Do all in 1981. Sometimes these worlds were quite separated in my life; but after I got clean and sober in 1990 I began to weave these worlds together. I teach Amazon mysteries which include physical empowerment through the martial arts, sexual empowerment for women to affirm their bodies and deepest desires, weaving together spiritual Sisterhood and empowerment in connection with the Goddess of 10,000 Names. You can read my blog at: http://masteramazon.blogspot.com.

Melitta Benu is a fledgling writer and sometime artist who focuses mostly on nekromantia, the Underworld gods and reviving their worship. Sooner or later, she'll get around to working on her website and her book about Persephone, but for the moment she is buried under the weight of graduate school. *Vae mihi!* Melitta's work can also be seen in *Bearing Torches*, Neos Alexandria's Hekate Devotional.

Rebecca Buchanan is the editor-in-chief of Bibliotheca Alexandrina. She is also the editor and web mistress of Eternal Haunted Summer, a Pagan literary ezine. She has been published in *Day Star and Whirling Wheel: A Devotional in Honor of Sunne, Goddess of the Sun and Mani, God of the Moon; Waters of Life: A Devotional in Honor of Isis and Serapis,* and many other collections. Her website is www.eternalhauntedsummer.com, and her email is baeditor@gmail.com.

Shirl Sazynski believes in the power of words, symbols and images to transform our lives through shared experience. She writes and illustrates magic realist stories for a variety of media. Her work appears in the upcoming Viethegame.com, and has been featured in literary magazines and anthologies including *Eternal Haunted Summer, Jabberwocky, Cargoes, String* and *Mythic Delirium.* Journalism, art and words can be found at shirlsazynski.com.

Sophie Reicher has studied the occult arts for two decades. She specializes in teaching Psychic and Spiritual Protection, ritual basics, and the fundamentals of meditation. While a practicing Northern Traditionalist, she maintains devotional practices to several Deities outside of that tradition, of Whom Ereshkigal is One. Her work has appeared in L. Black's *Crown of Violets*, G. Krasskova's *Day Star and Whirling Wheel* and *Runes: Theory and Practice*, and the online journal Blood for the Divine (bloodfordivine.blogspot.com). She has a forthcoming book on spiritual protection through New Page Books. To learn more, please visit her website at sreicher.weebly.com.

Janet Munin is a priestess of Ereshkigal and a student of hermetic magic and Qabalah. She has a Masters Degree in Comparative Religion and is a spiritual director in private practice. You can contact her at janet.munin@earthlink.net.

About the Bibliotheca Alexandrina

Ptolemy Soter, the first Makedonian ruler of Egypt, established the library at Alexandria to collect all of the world's learning in a single place. His scholars compiled definitive editions of the Classics, translated important foreign texts into Greek, and made monumental strides in science, mathematics, philosophy and literature. By some accounts over a million scrolls were housed in the famed library, and though it has long since perished due to the ravages of war, fire, and human ignorance, the image of this great institution has remained as a powerful inspiration down through the centuries.

To help promote the revival of traditional polytheistic religions we have launched a series of books dedicated to the ancient gods of Greece and Egypt. The library is a collaborative effort drawing on the combined resources of the different elements within the modern Hellenic and Kemetic communities, in the hope that we can come together to praise our gods and share our diverse understandings, experiences and approaches to the divine.

A list of our current and forthcoming titles can be found on the following page. For more information on the Bibliotheca, our submission requirements for upcoming devotionals, or to learn about our organization, please visit us at **neosalexandria.org**.

Sincerely,

The Editorial Board of the Library of Neos Alexandria

Current Titles from the Bibliotheca Alexandrina:

Written in Wine: A Devotional Anthology for Dionysos
Dancing God: Poetry of Myths and Magicks by Diotima
Goat Foot God by Diotima
Longing for Wisdom: The Message of the Maxims by Allyson Szabo
The Phillupic Hymns by P. Sufenas Virius Lupus
Unbound: A Devotional Anthology for Artemis
Waters of Life: A Devotional Anthology for Isis and Serapis
Bearing Torches: A Devotional Anthology for Hekate
Queen of the Great Below: An Anthology in Honor of Ereshkigal

Forthcoming Titles from the Bibliotheca Alexandrina:

Megaloi Theoi: A Devotional for the Dioskouroi and Their Families
From Cave to Sky: A Devotional Anthology for Zeus
*Anointed: A Devotional Anthology for the Deities of the Near and
    Middle East.*

50364965R00070

Made in the USA
Lexington, KY
12 March 2016